KV-638-187

ANGRY BABY!

ARTHUR MATHEWS has written for television since the early 1990s. Among the shows he has created and/or written (many with co-writer Graham Linehan) are *Father Ted*, *Hippies*, *Big Train*, *Toast Of London*, *The All New Alexei Sayle Show*, *Paris*, *Brass Eye*, *Harry Enfield And Chums*, *The Fast Show*, *Black Books*, *Val Falvey TD*; the film *Wide Open Spaces*; and the musical *I, Keano*.

He has written a 'memoir', *Well Remembered Days*, as well as T*he Craggy Island Parish Newsletters*, *Father Ted – The Complete Scripts* (with Graham Linehan) and *The Book Of Poor Ould Fellas* (with Declan Lynch).

ANGRY BABY!

IRELAND'S YOUNGEST POLITICAL
ACTIVIST SPEAKS OUT

KATIE WOODS

(WITH THE HELP OF ARTHUR MATHEWS)

HACHETTE
BOOKS
IRELAND

First published in 2012 by Hachette Books Ireland
A division of Hachette UK Ltd

Copyright © 2012 Arthur Mathews

A CIP catalogue record for this title is available from the British Library.

ISBN 978 1 444 74328 9

Inside design and typeset by Sin É Design
Cover design by AmpVisual.com
Cover and interior photos and
baby face illustration © Arthur Mathews
Other interior illustrations © istockphoto.

Printed and bound by Clays Ltd, St Ives plc
Hachette Books Ireland policy is to use papers that are natural, renewable
and recyclable products and made from wood grown in sustainable forests.
The logging and manufacturing processes are expected to conform to the
environmental regulations of the country of origin.

Hachette Books Ireland
8 Castlecourt Centre
Castleknock
Dublin 15, Ireland

A division of Hachette UK Ltd
338 Euston Road
London NW1 3BH

www.hachette.ie

Katie would like to dedicate this
book to her parents.

9 FEBRUARY 2010
Born.

10 FEBRUARY 2010
Can't really get my head around anything. Hear first complaint about bad weather. What is 'weather'?

11 FEBRUARY 2010
Drooling (not much fun), snoozing (nice), mewling (not sure about this). Every cliché in the book, basically!

12 FEBRUARY 2010

Right … I am in 'Ireland'. Therefore, I am 'Irish'. It 'comes with a lot of baggage', apparently. Don't know what this means, as have no understanding of literal or metaphorical meaning of the word 'baggage'. (Also not clear what 'literal' and 'metaphorical' mean. But I like the sound of them.) Other words I like the sound of: 'furry'; 'milk'; 'Wheeeeeeee!!'; '*zzzzzzzzzz*'.

Not sure if last two are actual words.

13 FEBRUARY 2010

Had *massive* sleep yesterday!!

14 FEBRUARY 2010

Home!! … To a place I've never been before. (So, not sure why it's 'home'.) Presume this will make some sense when I develop more brain power. Over fireplace (first one I've seen) are lots of cards, 'welcoming' me and congratulating bewildered-looking parents. I'm beginning to wonder how I 'came about'. Don't suppose I need to know the details for now. I'll put that one on the 'back burner' for the time being.

Hungry!

15 FEBRUARY 2010
Exhausted.

17 FEBRUARY 2010
Getting used to 'Ireland'. I fear I may have drawn a very, very short straw indeed. Climate: s**t. Economic climate: s**t. Dada compared the contents of my nappy to 'the mess the politicians have got us into'.

18 FEBRUARY 2010
Who is 'Seanie FitzPatrick'? The 'Seanie' (childish name) suggests this is someone I could be friends with.

19 FEBRUARY 2010

Breast-feeding is kind of weird, but parents (actually, one parent) keen to stick with it so that I will turn out 'normal'.

20 FEBRUARY 2010

Suffered from a general feeling of unease (and some colic) today. Big street protests – lots of serious-looking people with placards – on the television. My first thought was that they must be protesting about the weather, but apparently it's about 'cutbacks'. (Not to be confused with 'cutting the ball back', e.g. 'Damian Duff neatly cut the ball back there, for Robbie Keane to slot home.') Anyway! 100,000 people on the streets, according to trade union organisers. (100 people, according to the Gardaí (police).) It doesn't really matter – both figures seem *huge* to me).

Overall impression: things clearly aren't 'right' with the country.

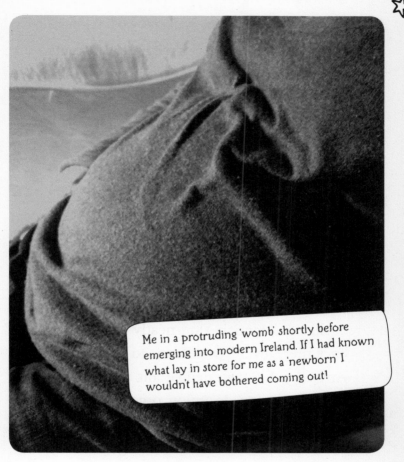

Me in a protruding 'womb' shortly before emerging into modern Ireland. If I had known what lay in store for me as a 'newborn' I wouldn't have bothered coming out!

21 FEBRUARY 2010

Picking up the 'basics' about Ireland, from hearing parents talking, and snippets on the television. Here's what I've learned so far:

- Until recently, the country was run by a Catholic Church.
- Fianna Fáil is the biggest political party. (Still getting to grips with word 'party', as it seems to have a few meanings. However, the term 'party atmosphere' seems to have little to do with Fianna Fáil.)
- Northern Ireland – strange place. A bit like Scotland, but much scarier.
- Anne Doyle – popular news reader.
- Everyone hates politicians and having to pay tax.

22 FEBRUARY 2010

I meet 'new people' when I go to a grim clinic to be weighed. (Average weight for 'newborn', apparently – no surprises.) Hear the word 'cutbacks' again – this time out of the mouth of a 'real' person (as opposed to the pretend people on television).

Before sleepy-time, Dada shows me insane footage on 'YouTube' (I like it!) of a man with three names ('David Davin-Power') at the Fianna Fáil 'Ard Fheis' (annual conference, apparently), surrounded by a bunch of 'party members'. Mama says it reminds her of a scene from a film called *The Birds*. They don't look like birds: I don't 'get' this. Might have something to do with the way they're standing around like stuffed parrots. There is clearly something **WRONG** with them.

23 FEBRUARY 2010

I find it a bit weird that Dada showed me that clip. It's very important that my senses aren't overloaded in these crucial early months of development. Showing me stuff like the Fianna Fáil Ard Fheis, where grown men stand around like parrots, could do me lasting damage.

24 FEBRUARY 2010

Have been given a cuddly toy as a present! He's white and he's a teddy, so I'm going to call him 'White Teddy'!

1 MARCH 2010

A new month! My first 'March'. Weather still awful. I literally don't know what sunlight looks like.

4 MARCH 2010

Strange – I called Mama 'NAMA' this morning. I don't really know what NAMA is, but there's been so much about it 'in the news' that I've started saying it a lot. Dada looked at their website, and it stands for 'National Asset Management Agency'. (In Irish: Gníomhaireacht Náisiúnta um Bhainistíocht Sócmhainní – I kid you not!) They have a nice picture of a harp as their logo, but Mama thinks it looks more like a barber's electronic razor, ready to give the country a good snip*. Things are looking ominous! (Please NAMA, don't cut back on Ella's Breakfast Food In Tubes for Babies! They look yummy!**)

5 MARCH 2010

First sighting of somebody called 'Bertie Ahern' on a documentary about 'great tyrants of the twentieth century', as Dada called it, half-jokingly. (It was actually a programme about Fianna Fáil.) Bertie is a sports columnist for the *News of the World*, but apparently he used to be An Taoiseach ('the leader'). Dada always goes friggin' berserk when he sees him. He calms down

---

* There is apparently a [new] 'Bored Snip' – a committee full of bored civil servants who unveiled a 'financial plan', which recommended areas for cutbacks in public spending in July 2009. More on this later: am not advanced enough brain-wise at the moment to get my head around it.

** For older babies only, apparently ('indigestible for newborns'), but I like the colours on the packet. I may develop a lifelong relationship with Ella's Breakfast Food (in tubes), similar to that which Liza Minnelli has with painkillers.

eventually and laughs, as he recalls the time that Bertie once said that he wanted to turn the trendy Temple Bar district into 'Dublin's West Bank'. The other West Bank is a Palestinian territory occupied by Israel since 1967 and a hotbed of internecine warfare,

My anxiety and foreboding is evident as I ponder the grim economic future which lies before me.

carnage and destruction. Presumably Bertie meant 'the Left Bank' – a hip area of Paris. According to Dada, this is more evidence that Bertie is a 'twerp' and 'doesn't know his a**e from his e***w'. An ad on TV for the NOTW featuring Bertie hiding in a fridge confused my little brain even further.

7 MARCH 2010

We all have to 'tighten our belts'. (I don't have a belt, but there's something on my nappy that's a bit like a belt: two paper flaps at the side with adhesive pads, which are affixed to the frontal part of the girdle. All this has the purpose of restraining any potential leakage or seepage – yeuch!) Mama wonders aloud (indelicately, as I'm in the room) about the possibility of making money out of me. She says I'd look good on the label of a bottle of baby food, or in baby wipes adverts on TV, faffing around with another bewildered, innocent-looking infant. Dada says I potentially look like the blonde girl who used to be on the Calvita cheese box. (I don't understand this reference – obviously before my time.) I wouldn't be surprised if Dada came up with an equally unsavoury plan to cynically exploit his first-born, by forcing me to write a book or something. (Probably involving his creepy fixation with Bertie Ahern.)

12 MARCH 2010

Apparently, Mama, like many of her generation (old people in their 30s), is a 'technophobe'. It took her about half an hour this morning to send a text, whereas even young children nowadays are 'computer literate' and just 'get it'.

I myself literally cannot imagine a world before the internet.

17 MARCH 2010

This day seems like some kind of celebration for eejits keen to forget the country's economic woes. I see lots of drunk eejits dressed up as leprechauns on the television. Mama explains that today is a celebration of Saint Patrick. She is 'slaving away' (her description), washing my baby clothes, but to pass the time 'explains' to me all about Saint Patrick. I'd heard about him before, and imagined him as a sporty type – 'Saint Patrick's Athletic'. But apparently this is a reference to a football club. We simply don't know if he was athletic or not, but these are things we do know about him (as 'explained' to me by Mama):

- Semi-mythical
- Welsh
- Captured by 'the Irish' and forced into slavery. (Is this kind of slavery related to washing clothes for babies?)
- Escaped from slavery by running away
- Returned to Britain

- Saw weird vision (drunk?)
- Converted 'the Irish' to Christianity
- Successfully marketed a previously useless horticultural product (the shamrock)
- Died

Later, on 'the news', the weirdest thing I've seen yet: lots of 'Saint Patrick's Day' parades featuring a whole load of eejits on the back of trucks. One from 'down the country' (where else?) featured a blacked-up man and some prostitutes representing the tribulations of playboy golfer Tiger Woods. I started crying at this – not because it was casual racism (which it CLEARLY was), but because it was stupid. 'Wait till she sees The Rose of Tralee,' Dada snorts at the TV. If this is the type of thing people do to forget the economic crisis, I'd prefer the economic crisis.

18 MARCH 2010

I am on a steep learning curve. Such a lot to take in, for a newly-born. Struggling with my frames of reference. (Not even sure what 'frames of reference' means.)

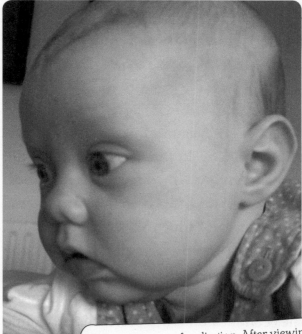

A stark moment of realisation. After viewing a Prime Time Special, I concur that the country is indeed 'f***ed'.

Very frustrating that my motor skills* are so poor. I don't think that Mama and Dada realise that behind the dribbling (literally) idiot they see before them is an articulate and thoughtful commentator on this world I've been born into.

19 MARCH 2010
Wind.

20 MARCH 2010
An 'ill wind' is blowing throughout the country. People are very unhappy with the current 'An Taoiseach', Brian Cowen, who took over from Bertie Ahern. I saw a photograph of him in the paper and was delighted (which I indicated by chuckling/gurgling sounds) to see that he looks just like a baby! (Except with hair and glasses.) His friends and family call him 'Biffo', after

---

* As opposed to 'motoring skills' – that means driving cars and trucks. Don't think I'd be allowed behind the wheel of a 4x4 Subaru just yet!

a cuddly bear in a comic for older children called *The Beano*, so this must mean that they like him. His 'popularity rating' as An Taoiseach is very low, though, so in order to get voters to 'give him their No. 1' (not sure what that means), he may have to give out free sweets and ice cream. I wish I was old enough to vote for him, because he really does look like a big baby!

22 MARCH 2010

'Enda' is the leader of the Opposition. (As in, 'opposed' to Brian 'Baby-Face' Cowen and the party he is the king of, Fianna Fáil. 'Enda' is ancient as hell, but looks 30 years younger. They say he might be the next An Taoiseach. He's from a place called Mayo, where nobody has ever been. He is very neat and tidy, and his mama obviously sends him off to the Dáil every day in a lovely suit and tie. He's very ANGRY in the Dáil, and I started to cry when I saw him yesterday on television because he was a bit frightening. Eventually I had to be taken out for a 15-mile walk in my pram. When I came back, I got upset again, when I saw a man in the paper who looked like the Devil. His name was Roooory Quinn. He's also a politician who lives in the Dáil.

28 MARCH 2010

Mama and Dada had a 'rough night' last night, and didn't bother with my regular 'bathtime for babies'. I am a member of the 'Great Unwashed'!

29 MARCH 2010

Apparently, the 'Great Unwashed' is also a term for ordinary people, of which I am one. I'm beginning to hear a lot about 'the anger of the ordinary people', or 'the fury of the ordinary man in the street' (not sure who he is). Anyway, seemingly everybody is FURIOUS at the politicians and the bankers for getting us in this mess. I'm beginning to wonder if there's anything I can do to help change things, despite my lack of language, motor skills and (let's face it) experience. It occurs to me that I am becoming 'politically aware'! I want *more* than just food and sleep and hugs! I am a DEMANDING BABY!

It seems that in 'the olden days', if people felt strongly about a political or economic issue, they'd either organise marches and protest against their enemies by holding big banners with slogans on them, or by killing them. Now, everybody writes 'blogs'. According to Dada, a 'blog' is something written by 'socially inadequate, egotistical losers who get their kicks by sending out their half-baked, solipsistic ramblings to anyone who accidentally comes across them via an absent-minded google'. Hey, I could get into that!

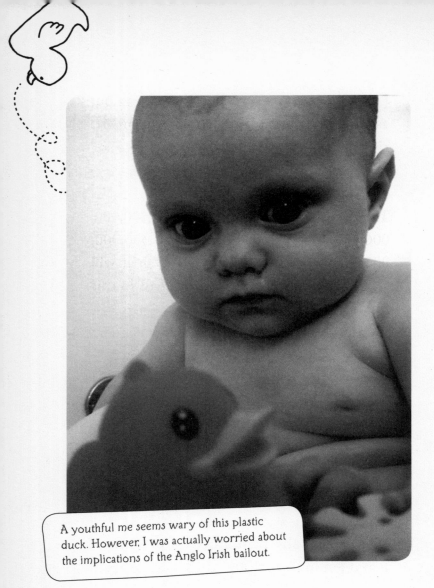

A youthful me seems wary of this plastic duck. However, I was actually worried about the implications of the Anglo Irish bailout.

I can almost say 'Google'!! (It's coming out as 'Guggle' at the moment, but I'm on the right track!)

1 APRIL 2010

The country needs €9,000,000,000,000,000,000,000,000,000,000,000,000,000,000,000,000,000,000,000,000,000,000,000,000,000,000,000,000, or it will go bust!! I cannot yet count to two, so this figure is truly mind-boggling.

2 APRIL 2010

Apparently that figure I quoted yesterday was an April Fool's joke printed in a magazine called *Ireland's Own*. The actual figure is only €9,000,000,000,000,000,000,000,000,000,000,000,000,000,000,000,000,000,000,000,000,000,000,000,000. Still, it looks rather a LOT!

3 APRIL 2010

It seems that I live in 'Dublin 6', which means I will grow up with a nice accent suitable for reading traffic reports and updates on the early morning RTÉ radio news. (Key word: 'southbound'.)

6 APRIL 2010

Still getting used to parents. It's a slow process.

Mama: cuddly, protective, clichéd 'working-mother-balancing-career-with-childcare' type.

Dada: sits around watching television (big colourful thing in the corner of living room!) and complaining – mostly about 'the state of the country'. Prematurely balding – but this doesn't make him baby-like, just 'old'. Seems to have 'issues'.

I know I'm supposed to 'like' them, but ...

10 APRIL 2010

Unemployment up by 3,000 this month. Unsure if that includes me.

11 APRIL 2010

I feel HELPLESS (even by baby standards), because I am unable to do anything about the financial mess. I'm just lost in my own thoughts, unable to articulate what I think. I can only cry and scream, and kick up a fuss. (I know Joe Higgins does this too, but, as well as being able to form actual words, he has people to hand out leaflets.) I can't wait to be able to SPEAK! After all, it is *my* future at stake in all this!

13 APRIL 2010

Have decided that pink is my favourite colour. It's just ... fluffy! (I wish White Teddy was pink!*)

---

* Although then he would probably have to be renamed 'Pink Teddy'.

14 APRIL 2010

Dada and Mama are always around the house. (I find this slightly sinister.) She is on maternity leave, and I think he does something in 'the media' – possibly a 'film maker'.

16 APRIL 2010

Nappy changing is a bore. While Mama was struggling with the Pampers, she had something called *Liveline with Joe Duffy* on the radio. Lots of eejits ring up to annoy the poor presenter, who pretends to be interested in their stupid opinions. The general 'gist' of today's conversation was 'ALL BANKERS SHOULD BE PUT IN JAIL OR POSSIBLY HANGED'. I am swept along by the tide of anger and frustration, and am so grumpy,* I almost fall off the changing table!

---

* Not sure if this is the right word. It should be whatever Joe Higgins is.

17 APRIL 2010

What kind of country have I been born into?! Apparently a former An Taoiseach, 'Charlie Hockey', stole €250,000 from one of his friends from a fund that was supposed to make his friend a new liver!

18 APRIL 2010

I learn something new every day. Today I learnt that cows say 'Moo! Moo!', and that in the first quarter of 2009, GDP was down 8.5 per cent on the same quarter the previous year, and GNP down 12 per cent. Unemployment is up 8.75 per cent, to 11.4 per cent. The economy exited recession in the third quarter of 2009, with GDP growing by 0.3 per cent in the quarter, but GNP continued to contract – by 1.4 per cent. Now, I have no head for maths, but this all seems like VERY BAD NEWS INDEED.

20 APRIL 2010

I keep hearing the name 'Anglo Irish Bank'. I think 'Anglo Irish' are Protestant people who live in Ireland, but who have English accents. They probably don't trust real Irish banks, like the Bank of Ireland or Allied Irish Bank, because they're run by Irish people. From what I've seen of Irish people so far, I can understand this!

21 APRIL 2010

Finding out about how banks work. Today Mama showed me a thing called a 'piggy bank'. What this is, basically, is a pig (not a real pig – it looked like it was made out of rubber or something, and I was quite excited because it's my favourite colour – pink!) … Sorry, that sentence was waaaay too long, and I'm getting confused. Will start again. Anyway, it's a pink pig (not a real one), with a slot in its back that you put coins in. I (or more realistically, Mama) could put coins in it, until I have saved up enough for a nice toy or some baby clothes. Real banks work a bit like that, except if you put enough coins in, they will eventually pay you 'interest'. Also, if you have no coins at all, *they* can give you some, and *you* will end up paying *them* 'interest'. During the 'Celtic Tiger' (not an actual tiger), banks would give you **LOADS** of piggy banks full of coins and you wouldn't have to pay them back for **AGES**. Hence, the country was **RUINED!**

Searching for the Financial Section in the Sunday newspapers can become a little frustrating!

22 APRIL 2010

My potential friend Seanie FitzPatrick apparently loaned himself a piggy bank that had *84 million Euros' worth of coins* in it! He was head of the Anglo Irish Bank (for Protestants), and didn't tell anyone about it. I don't want to be (potential) friends with him any more.

24 APRIL 2010

Found out more about the 'Celtic Tiger'. As I mentioned earlier, not an actual tiger. It refers to a time when everyone in Ireland was happy and the country would regularly win the Eurovision song contest. Not sure how this relates to a tiger.

25 APRIL 2010

Baby-like An Taoiseach Brian Cowen's popularity rating down to zero per cent. He has gone slightly up since last week, when at one stage he was at *minus* 4 per cent. I wonder if other babies are as unhappy about the situation as I am? It's hard to tell with babies, because we can't talk, and do so much faffing around and falling over.

1 MAY 2010

Teeth. Weird! I don't need teeth at the moment, do I? Still breast-feeding. (Awkward, not to say embarrassing for both of us, if teeth come into it.)

False alarm! I'm too young to have teeth. It was a 'phantom' tooth, one which I imagined. Very common in infants as we 'expand' our brains and begin to imagine all kinds of things. Closely linked to paranoia – which is a bit of a worry.*

13 MAY 2010

Big news! I am to have a 'childminder'! Not at all concerned about this, as, to be honest, am getting slightly bored with Mama and

---

* Am I being paranoid here?

Dada. I regard myself as an outgoing, effervescent and 'bouncing' (though not literally!) baby, who gets on really well with strangers. In later life, I fully expect to blossom into a 'bubbly personality': someone who 'lights up the room every time she enters'. (Dada has noted, rather ominously, that these descriptions are often applied to murder victims!)

Anyway! *My very own childminder*! Am excited by the possibility of MORE CUDDLES!

14 MAY 2010

Potential childminders are being auditioned. Three ladies called round today, and Dada and Mama gave them 'the once-over'. It was a bit like the *X-Factor*. The three ladies could all be described as 'buxom', which is great from my point of view because I think cuddling is enhanced by big bazookas. (After cuddling, I would list 'nestling' as one of my absolute favourite things to do.) Ideally, I would have liked to audition the ladies for their nestling capacities, to see who was the most snug ('snuggest'?), but Dada and Mama were more interested in 'working hours' and 'transport issues'. Dada seemed to prefer the most 'buxom' of the three, who was also the youngest and prettiest, and came from Sweden. Mama, for some reason, preferred the fattest (is it 'fat-ist' to say 'fattest', I wonder?) and oldest of the ladies, who comes from Swinford in Mayo* (where 'Enda' comes from). The other contestant was disqualified on the grounds that she wanted too much money.

15 MAY 2010

The successful candidate is unveiled! It is to be 46-year-old Siobhan Devlin from Swinford! (Now living in Swords, but says she doesn't mind the drive in.) Dada is disappointed that it's not going to be 19-year-old Inge from Stockholm, but

---

* It is now suspected that at some point in the recent past, Mayo closed down, and everyone left and went to Dublin.

Mama told him frankly that he was never going to win that argument.

Greece has collapsed.*

16 MAY 2010

Already Mama and Dada are talking about 'potential schools'. A few years ago everyone went to places run by the Catholic Church, but since it was revealed that every single child who ever went to a Catholic school was 'abused'**(?), the race is now on to send kids to 'non-denominational' schools run by atheists and Protestants.*** Anyway, I'm not concerned about that at the moment, because a) it's years away, and b) it may not be relevant, as Ireland is facing imminent

---

* Was confused when I first heard this on the news. I had an image of big buildings like the Acropolis falling down, and everything ending up in the sea. However, I discovered via a tweet by the Greek Minister for Finance that it referred to an economic collapse. (How boringly predictable. No doubt the bankers are responsible.)

** 'Don't go there'.

*** Different Protestants from the ones running Anglo Irish Bank, presumably.

collapse and may be wound up and sold off to the highest bidder.

20 MAY 2010

My first day with Siobhan Devlin! She read me a few stories (princes, dogs, castles, caterpillars, etc.) and I crawled around a bit. She was nice and there were *excellent* cuddles! I LOVE HER!

Hillary Clinton circa 1979. My babysitter/manager, Siobhan Devlin, looks like an older, frumpier version of this.

22 MAY 2010

Siobhan Devlin is a bit 'New Age-y'. She believes in horoscopes and claims to be something called a 'baby whisperer'. That means she can understand what babies mean when they gurgle and generally make incomprehensible sounds, which other adults think are gibberish. She told Mama all this, and 'Mater' nodded at her politely, but I can read the old lady well enough to know that she secretly thought Siobhan Devlin was a bit of a 'Loo-Laa' (who may also be one of the Teletubbies?). Her secret thoughts were confirmed later on, when she said to Dada, 'I think Siobhan Devlin is a bit of a "Loo-Laa".'

23 MAY 2010

Even if Siobhan Devlin is a bit of a 'Loo-Laa', I think there is something in this 'baby whispering' thing. I indicated this morning that I wanted some formula milk from the fridge. ('Indicated' is hardly the correct word – I half-gesticulated, half-screamed, grabbed a nappy flamboyantly and put it on my head, then wet myself.) I wasn't even that thirsty, and to be honest, formula milk tastes almost as bad as that UHT shit (which I was once given accidentally), but I thought I'd test Siobhan Devlin. To my surprise (and delight) Siobhan Devlin fetched the milk from the fridge and gave it to me, saying something like, 'This is what you want, isn't it, little baby?'! I could have done without the patronising tone, but I immediately found myself thinking, 'At last! Somebody who UNDERSTANDS me!'

27 MAY 2010

Siobhan Devlin's mother has been in a hospital corridor (yes, a hospital CORRIDOR, not a hospital), after suffering a broken leg in a fall from a giraffe at Fota Island Wildlife Park (don't ask), so my childminder has gone away for a few days. Mama is less than pleased about this, as she has to come home from work to mind me.

Even I, a 3½-month-old child, can see that it's utterly DISGRACEFUL that a 90-year-old woman who has just tumbled off a giraffe has to lie around in a corridor because of the shortage of beds in our hospitals. (Incidentally, the giraffe had to be humanely put down* after the incident.) I blame the politicians!

28 MAY 2010

White Teddy and I saw a lovely old man called Fintan O'Toole on television. He was 'debating' economic issues with politicians (boo!) and a woman with long blonde hair and huge eyes. I found the points he made persuasive and convincing. If he ever founded a political party for similarly concerned people, I'd probably join up.

---

* Put down by humans, presumably?

(Especially if they had a youth/toddler/baby wing.)

3 JUNE 2010

I was VERY EXCITED to see that there is a copy of Fintan O'Toole's *Ship of Fools: How Stupidity and Corruption Sank the Celtic Tiger* on the bookshelf in the living room! (An unwanted gift?) I embarked on an absolute onslaught of tantrums/petulance/screaming and other 'baby wiles' to try and make Mama understand that I needed to see this book. But no luck – they just thought I was hungry. Damn!

Portugal has collapsed.*

(No doubt the bankers are responsible.)

---

* Was confused when I first heard this on the news. I had an image of big buildings like the Lisbon Stadium of Light football ground falling down, and everything ending up in the sea. However, I discovered via a tweet by the Portuguese Minister for Finance that it referred to an economic collapse. (How boringly predictable.)

4 JUNE 2010

Great! The Baby Whisperer is back! I hardly had to do anything (just a short burst of persistent, high-pitched baby-grunting) to make Siobhan Devlin know that I wanted to look at *Ship of Fools: How Stupidity and Corruption Sank the Celtic Tiger* by Fintan O'Toole. Not only did she get it down off the bookshelf, but then SHE STARTED READING IT TO ME! I was literally wetting myself with excitement. This 'baby whispering' thing is for real!

Unlike most things I've read (til now), there were no farms or ducks or moo-moo cows, but I soon got over my disappointment. This was a different type of book altogether, which didn't even have any 'pop-up' features. Neither were there funny noises, such as bells and trampoline sounds, instigated at the pressing of a picture. Instead, Siobhan Devlin read a particularly vitriolic chapter on 'the bankers'. Fintan really sticks it to them, and, yes, I WAS angry after hearing what they've done to our beloved country. When Siobhan Devlin told the folks later how animated I'd become listening to Fintan's wise words, Mama said to Dada that I must like the book because of the nice cartoon drawing on the cover (of a 'Euro' drowning in a river!). But no.

Contemplating the prospect of early emigration. At any moment, I half-expected to be wheeled in my buggy to the ferry terminal at Dún Laoghaire.

What I liked about it was O'Toole's forensic exposure of clientelism, malpractice and cynicism amongst the country's ruling elite.

5 JUNE 2010

I wish I could read, but for the moment I'm more than happy with Siobhan Devlin doing the spadework for me. She knows instinctively how interested I am in the economic situation of the country and how keen I am to learn from Fintan. I LOVE Siobhan Devlin! (Mama and Dada find my keen interest in *Ship of Fools: How Stupidity and Corruption Sank the Celtic Tiger* amusing. They must have thought I was a bit weird [in a baby way] to want to look at the book in the first place, but now realise that they can use this to impress their friends, in an ironic fashion: 'Better get Katie wised up to what these f***ers are up to)!'

6 JUNE 2010

More tooth fantasies. Surely one will pop up sooner or later.

7 JUNE 2010

I like those painkillers, given to babies for minor ailments, in liquid form (usually pink), that you drink from a small white plastic spoon. I get a bit of a 'buzz' off them. Apologies – I'm babbling. I mean, literally. I'm babbling: it's what happens at 4 months. I'm trying to say words, but even though I know what I'm trying to say, they come out like gobbledygook. A bit like Brian Cowen on a radio programme after a late night. (Sorry – couldn't resist obvious joke!) 'Gobbledygook' is a classic 'babble' word. Also, 'Ballydehob', 'Bord Gáis' (actually two words) and 'Caoimghín Ó Caoláin' (also two – and possibly even three? – words).

'Here's another teaser for you this morning – what do you call male ballerinas? Just a question, nothing in it for you. [*Dramatic mock puzzlement, mixed with air of mystery.*] What do you call male ballerinas?

'*... I'm going to play that for Jan – Jan O'Meara in Ballycotton. God bless ya! Because I know you like that. It'd be actually a good idea, I'm just thinking, Jan – when you see Ennio Morricone live in St Mark's Square in Venice – if you have the telly on and sit in the back garden, and close your eyes, you'd be away ... With the way the weather is, you could pretend to be away, and listen to it and watch it – or I don't know, just turn off the old head, no harm at all in doing it from time to time if you* [putting on accent – Cockney?] *get the opportunity, really no harm ...*'

What the HELL was that!? Mama was listening to the news on the radio, but Dada thought it was so grim, he tuned it to Lyric fm. Apparently 'that' was *Marty Whelan in the Morning*. I think I preferred the news!

15 JUNE 2010
A sleepless night for Mama and Dada. I cry ALL night, from dusk til dawn. Why? Because the Economic and Social Research Institute has predicted an economic contraction of 14 per cent by the end of the year.

16 JUNE 2010
Mama took me to see a friend of hers who has a baby called Bernard (7 months). I didn't care much for Bernard, I'm afraid. He sat there listless, unable (or unwilling) to do anything for himself, bringing nothing to the conversation (which was mostly on the subject of the television programme *Desperate Housewives*), and generally acting as if he really didn't give a damn. Is this what the next generation is going to

be like? Complacent and apathetic? What about the 'baby boomers'* of the 1960s, who rioted in Paris and protested about Vietnam? I HATE the attitude of babies like Bernard. They are far too reliant on the older generation to do things for them. If only I could organise babies into a pressure group to make the politicians aware that the younger generation are going to fight back!

17 JUNE 2010

I'm pretty sure that Siobhan Devlin can sense my political radicalism. Shane Ross was on the radio and I literally howled in agreement when he demanded action against the bankers. 'Do you hate the bankers too?' she asked me, but not in a jokey way. She was deadly serious. I was deadly serious too. I could feel a 'moment' between us.

---

* Not actual babies. Somewhat confusing.

People are saying Spain could be the next country to collapse.*

22 JUNE 2010

Last night I again woke up in a rage (mostly about the state of the country – but also due to some wind). Mama and Dada were watching a DVD downstairs, so I was brought into the sitting room for some unscheduled family viewing time until I calmed down a bit. The film on the DVD was called *The Diving Bell and the Butterfly*, and was about a man who couldn't be bothered speaking (I think this was what was going on – I missed the beginning), but could communicate by blinking. It was a revelatory moment: maybe *I* could communicate by frantic blinking! I tried

---

* Was confused when I first heard this on the news. I had an image of big buildings like the Del Prado Museum falling down, and everything ending up in the sea. However, I discovered via a tweet by the Spanish Minister for Finance that it referred to an economic collapse. (How boringly predictable. No doubt the bankers are responsible.)

it, but of course the parents missed the whole point of what I was doing, and I was soon packed off to bed again after a bit of perfunctory temperature-taking via thermometer in ear. (Any time I show any signs of unusual behaviour, they stick that thing into me. Apparently it can be shoved in other places besides ears!)

Tomorrow, I shall try the blinking again – with Siobhan Devlin.

23 JUNE 2010

Siobhan Devlin knew what I was trying to achieve with the frantic blinking! She said, 'I know you're trying to communicate by frantic blinking, but I can understand you anyway. I'm a baby whisperer, remember?' I LOVE YOU, SIOBHAN DEVLIN!

30 JUNE 2010

Just the usual baby stuff recently – being taken out for walks in pram, basic eating

(I'm *so* uncoordinated!), nappy changing (boring/distasteful), hiccupping, drooling …

Mama and Dada read me 'baby' books, by which I'm rather bored. Some of them don't even have hard covers, and are all floppy. There are even plastic ones I can take into the bath with me (pointless). I have books called *Shapes* and *Colours,* which are 'about' … shapes and colours. Honestly, it's beyond basic. Circles, squares, triangles, hexagons (a bit more sophisticated, but surely one of the most useless shapes: why does anything need SIX sides?) … Red, blue, yellow, etc. Hmm … I have no real opinion on colours. Apart from pink (which I LOVE, probably because I'm a baby girl*), they really do seem much of a muchness. I know that it's true that 'everything is not black and white' (a phrase I heard used recently by Baby-Face

---

* On reflection, I realise that associating pink with girls is insultingly sexist. I like pink because it's pink. End of.

Cowen), but surely there is no need for beige?

Mostly I sit there glumly as I'm being read these books, longing for the return of Siobhan Devlin, who – when Mama and Dada are safely out of the house – reads me more of *Ship of Fools: How Stupidity and Corruption Sank the Celtic Tiger*.

I'm silently pondering Fintan's many innovative ideas and sound strategies, when it's time for Siobhan Devlin to leave. And I'm still trying to absorb sensible proposals such as – 'Before an election, a civic movement has to create a critical mass around the idea of radical political reform' – when Dada comes in and begins to play 'Upside-Down World'. This involves him turning me upside down and then flopping me on to my belly. Boring, predictable and not without risk of injury.

1 JULY 2010

Chocolate and crisps look nice.

Me with some baby-toy contraption. I was wishing it was a time machine, so I could travel back to the 'Celtic Tiger' years!

2 JULY 2010

Apparently I'm 'not allowed' chocolate and crisps. Will pretend to feed them to White Teddy instead.

4 JULY 2010

Had fun pretending to 'feed' chocolate and crisps to White Teddy! None went into his mouth, but there was a hell of a lot of 'brown smearing', which was naughty but at the same time, tremendous fun.

Some Siobhan Devlin news: it appears that she looks after a few more babies. A 1-year-old in Rathmines called Jack (all boy-babies these days seem to be called Jack), and a girl-toddler in Harold's Cross called Aoife. This information emerged when Siobhan Devlin was chatting to Mama in the kitchen. I've noticed that they have a bunch of topics which they seem to natter about all the time. These are:

1. How useless men are;
2. *Desperate Housewives;*
3. The viewing figures of the *Late Late Show* (like the stock markets, always going up and down);
4. Shopping, with special reference to the Lidl and Aldi supermarket chains.

5. Of course, I hear the odd remark about how useless the bankers and politicians are, but generally, any serious analysis in the manner of Fintan O'Toole is clearly not on the agenda. This is the typical mood when my parents are chatting too. I fear that Mama and Dada are typical of the majority of people in the country – happy to just 'give out' about things and not do anything about them. I despair.

6 JULY 2010

Siobhan Devlin has been telling me about the other babies she looks after – Jack Redmond and Aoife Clarke. What she has to say gladdens my heart. They too are FURIOUS about what is happening in the country, and, like me, are big fans of *Ship of Fools: How Stupidity and Corruption Sank the Celtic Tiger*. Aoife Clarke even went on a protest march! (Didn't get precise details of this – presumably she was accompanied by 'minders' of some sort.) According to Siobhan Devlin, Jack Redmond disagrees slightly with some aspects of Fintan's analysis, but is generally in agreement, that 'something needs to be done'. I must meet these babies!

8 JULY 2010

By a stroke of luck, Siobhan Devlin has requested to take me to Aoife Clarke's house tomorrow! This is because Aoife Clarke's mother is going through a messy divorce (I bet not as messy though as the particularly foul nappy I did this morning as a result of eating a pile of fruit), and needs to swap days so she can see her solicitor. Mama agreed, and I am now *rather* excited at the prospect of meeting a fellow child-radical.

9 JULY 2010

Occasionally a person can meet another person, and there is an immediate 'connection'. This is what happened yesterday with me and Aoife Clarke. Siobhan Devlin collected me in the morning and wheeled me over to Harold's Cross in the buggy. At the front door, I heard excitable 'baby noises' from within, and it was clear that whoever was about to be revealed was as keen to meet me as I was to meet them. When the door opened, I was not disappointed. Before me was a rather angelic-looking toddler, who ressembled one of those weird kids in America that are entered into child beauty pageants by their equally strange parents. However, it soon became apparent that, despite her near-perfect appearance, Aoife Clarke was as down-to-earth as Maureen Potter or The Corrs (except for Jim Corr). Both Siobhan Devlin and Aoife Clarke's Mama immediately launched into a succession of gushing exclamations such as, 'They like each other!'; 'Look, they're giving each other a kiss!'; 'Aren't they sweet together?', etc. Early exchanges between my new acquaintance and me were appropriately playful and friendly (yet feisty!). Within five minutes, I hit Aoife Clarke with a (toy) brick, and she responded by emptying the contents of a baby water container over me. It was clear that we were going to have tremendous fun together, and the four hours I spent in the house went by in an instant. I felt it must have been like the first time that Martin Amis met Christopher Hitchens: a lifelong friendship was about to be embarked upon. Happily, I noticed that the (broken) Clarke household boasted a copy of *Ship of Fools: How Stupidity and Corruption Sank the Celtic Tiger* on its bookshelf. And then, after we shared half a banana between us, my joy was complete:

Siobhan Devlin started to read extracts from Fintan's wonderful book aloud to two attentive and contented little babies. **THERE IS SOMETHING GOING ON HERE!**

Aoife Clarke

11 JULY 2010

I'm not sure if I can honestly say I 'met' Jack Redmond today, but I certainly caught a glimpse of him. His Mama had to drop by to give Siobhan Devlin keys (I've noticed this type of thing goes on a lot with grown-ups), and I saw him through the kitchen window. He was sitting in the car seat in the back (similar to the one I use, purchased from Tony Kealy's in Walkinstown), and he smiled at me. I think he must have known who I was! I have a strong feeling that Siobhan Devlin has been discussing my growing political awareness with him, as well as with Aoife Clarke.

12 JULY 2010

Some kind of funny-looking fancy dress parades in Northern Ireland today, shown on the news. Weird! It's such a genuinely strange place.

14 JULY 2010

A fascinating discussion on television last night about the economy in crisis, featuring the 'Big Three': Fintan, David McWilliams

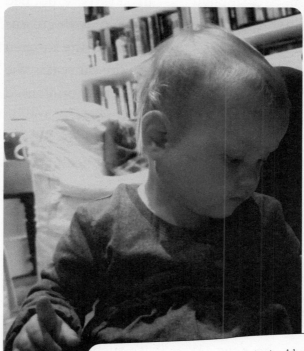

'Wait a moment! These figures don't add up!' Studying Fianna Fáil's plan for economic recovery (out of shot).

and Shane Ross* – all under the watchful, nanny-like gaze of that frighteningly tall woman with the long blonde hair and huge eyes. I was supposed to be asleep but made a tremendous fuss, so 'the folks' had little choice but to take me down to the living room. I couldn't help wondering if Aoife Clarke and Jack Redmond were also watching …

Hell's Bells!!

18 JULY 2010

Overheard a conversation between Mama and Siobhan Devlin this morning. Siobhan Devlin was saying that BOTH Aoife Clarke and Jack Redmond have been acting up a lot recently. I immediately wondered if, like me, they'd deliberately set out to make a fuss by staging screaming/hissy fits, thus leaving

---

* While Senator Ross was speaking, Dada launched into a tirade about him being 'a stockbroker and a cheerleader for Anglo Irish when it was popular', and 'a general know-it-all'.

their parents with little choice but to take them down to the living room, where they'd be able to watch the big TV debate between Ross, McWilliams and O'Toole. I think they did, you know. I really think they did.

21 JULY 2010

Am seriously considering forming a loose organisation of disaffected babies. There are lots of practical problems, of course, but people like Gandhi and Hitler had to start somewhere. At the moment, there is myself, Aoife Clarke and probably Jack Redmond, all under the care of super Baby Whisperer, Siobhan Devlin.

Also, as a matter of urgency, after Dada's informative tirade against Shane Ross, I have done a comprehensive and exhaustive background check on Fintan. He was never a stockbroker, isn't from Mayo and has never taken part in a St Patrick's Day parade. And I like his hair (as does White Teddy). Phew, relief!

22 JULY 2010

Siobhan Devlin definitely 'gets' what I'm up to. Today she did something odd, yet rather brilliant. She had the very exciting idea that I could start a 'baby blog' and post it on the internet. Siobhan Devlin reckons that she is so 'in tune' with me that she can compose it, and I can agree or disagree with what she comes up with, by using my 'basic motor skills'. We haven't discussed this in detail (partly because my motor skills are, indeed, basic), but I can indicate agreement by laughing my head off, or disagreement via the old standbys of hysterical screaming/crying, etc.

EXCITING!

23 JULY 2010

Siobhan Devlin has come up with a name for my baby blog! It's called *veryangrybaby.com*, and now I/we have to compose my/our very first blog! EXTREMELY EXCITING!

24 JULY 2010

It's really amazing how 'in tune' with me Siobhan Devlin is! I sat with her at the laptop as she tapped away on the keyboard, and I hardly had to do any hysterical screaming at all. (I did a little, but that was because I suddenly became very hungry.) Within about 20 minutes, we had written our first blog! It would have taken even less time, but I was so excited that I required two nappy changes in quick succession. (I have *literally* never been so excited in my life!) Hunger! Nappy changes! A very emotional morning.

Here is 'the blog' in full:

'In 1916, the founders of Ireland pledged to "cherish all the children of the State", and make the new island one of the greatest places in the world. Now, that noble objective has been crushed by the recent dubious activities of the greedy bankers and unscrupulous politicians. It is time for the babies and young people (under fives) of Ireland to come together in unison, and say in one voice, "We are the future of this country and we demand strong leadership now – possibly under Fintan O'Toole." If there are any other babies who feel this way, or if you are a parent and believe that this is how your child feels, please leave feedback with this very angry baby.'

I feel AMAZING!!

25 JULY 2010

In the olden days (over five years ago), a child receiving 'hits' would almost certainly be attending a school being run by the Christian Brothers. But the 'hits' I have received refer to the number of people who have logged on to *veryangrybaby.com*! Sixty people have 'found' me, and some have even left some 'positive feedback'.

26 JULY 2010

The first 'negative feedback' … Someone has said I don't know what I'm talking about, and that my views are 'childish'. May have been left by some unhappy Fianna Fáiler. Depressed.

27 JULY 2010

I met Jack Redmond today. I say 'met', but it felt more like an official 'meet and greet', with a strange air of formality surrounding it. Like President McAleese meeting the Queen. It was all a bit unsatisfactory. About a minute after Siobhan Devlin introduced us (accompanied by the usual tedious, over-the-top, gushing *faux* baby talk from S.D. and J.R.'s mother – ENOUGH ALREADY!), Jack Redmond fell over, banged the back of his bonce, and started bawling VERY LOUDLY! This went on for what I thought was about half an hour, but which was in fact only ten seconds. (Something to do with time appearing to pass at a slower pace when experienced by very young children.) It was hard to know what Jack Redmond felt about the economic situation, though I was able to give him some of my baby analysis in the short periods when he wasn't blubbering like a particularly blubbery Brian Cowen.

A frustrating encounter.

28 JULY 2010

Mama knows about the blog. I heard her discussing it with Siobhan Devlin. She didn't seem unhappy. She may enjoy the 'notoriety', and see the possibility of making some money out of it. (Is that my 'cynical side' coming out?)

29 JULY 2010

A tiny baby called Tim Hanratty from Galway has been in touch. He is only 2 DAYS OLD – and yet took the time and trouble to congratulate me on starting the blog. He already claims to be 'disillusioned' with Ireland, and wishes he had been born somewhere else. (This is a common theme in a lot of the feedback I have received thus far – but that it should come from a super-young infant, who is less than a week old, is no less than heartbreaking!) Isn't it a bit weird that a tiny tot like him has got in touch? I presume he has a Siobhan Devlin-like childminder who 'interprets' his thoughts and communicates for him. Or, it could be some joker having a laugh at my expense. I am clearly an 'innocent abroad' in the blogging world, but, nevertheless, I am finding the experience intensely rewarding.

30 JULY 2010

Wrote another blog yesterday about recapitalisation and the collapse of the Irish banking system. Siobhan Devlin thinks that possibly this might go 'over the heads' of my mostly baby audience, so I'm going to do the next one about more obvious 'baby issues', such as intense sleeping, minor coughs and nappy rash.

31 JULY 2010

Some good feedback about yesterday's blog, especially my piece on nappy rash. Correspondents seem to like the idea that my comments are uniquely from the 'baby's point of view'. Interestingly, while I can obviously feel the intense discomfort of nappy rash, I don't actually know what it looks like. Most babies don't, of course, unless their parents undertake the peculiar practice of taking photographs of the affected region for the family album. (Siobhan Devlin told me that when her uncle died, she found amongst his possessions an album full of photos of close-ups of babies' bottoms affected by nappy rash. Her uncle was, of course, a Catholic priest.)

2 AUGUST 2010

Siobhan Devlin said that, in order to promote the blog, I should sign up to Twitter and Facebook. I instinctively know what these are, probably in a way that my parents, when children themselves, were familiar with fairies and goblins.

Rather annoyingly, there already is an 'Angry Baby' on Twitter. In fact there seem to be lots and lots of 'Angry Babies' on Twitter. I have a strong feeling though that these aren't real babies, but rather the disingenuous creations of parents with nothing better to do than set up false accounts for their mischievous sprogs. I have taken the name 'Concerned/Angry Baby' instead.

3 AUGUST 2010

Opened up my 'Concerned/Angry Baby' Twitter account, with the single word 'teething'. I got twelve retweets. Honestly, have people nothing better to do?

6 AUGUST 2010

Mama and Dada took me down to the chemist's today to get my first passport photo taken. Passport photos are SO embarrassing! I look about 3 days old in mine. I presume I'm getting a passport so that if things get really bleak on the economic front, we can all move to ANYWHERE ELSE IN THE WORLD to look for a job. There has already been talk of putting me on the labels of baby food and nappy packaging, etc. Dada again remarked on my (potential) similarity to the girl on the Calvita cheese boxes. I don't like being made to feel like a commodity! (I think Marx said something similar – although he wasn't specifically referring to me).

8 AUGUST 2010

I tweeted today that I have never used a soother and somebody got back to me, saying that I was being stuck-up and politically correct!

Sharing a joke with Jack Redmond (partly disguised for legal reasons). An early recruit for Babies for Change, we soon parted company over a disagreement on policy. Sadly, Jack (and his parents) were forced to emigrate to the UK due to the economic downturn.

9 AUGUST 2010

Dana is really boring.*

10 AUGUST 2010

Found out today that Jack Redmond has his own blog. Of course, it was Siobhan Devlin (who else?) who told me about it. Disappointingly, he is blogging about **ECONOMIC MATTERS** – surely my specialist area of baby expertise and my **UNIQUE SELLING POINT!** Jack Redmond's views on the economy are closely modelled on mine, which is even more annoying. It seems blindingly obvious to me that his opinions consist more or less exactly of the points I made during our short first meeting, simply rehashed by him. Any other observations he made were **TRULY BABYISH**.

---

* No particular context for this. Just a general observation. White Teddy agrees with me.

13 AUGUST 2010

Since it is Siobhan Devlin who is 'channelling' Jack Redmond's thoughts and typing them up for him, I voiced to her my displeasure at his blog. Surely he can come up with something a bit more original?

15 AUGUST 2010

Is Jack Redmond a neo-con?

16 AUGUST 2010

Wrong of me to suggest that Jack Redmond is a neo-con, as I don't know what a neo-con is.

17 AUGUST 2010

EXTREMELY uncomfortable nappy rash today. If not literally a pain in the arse, a definite pain *around* the arse. It happened on Siobhan Devlin's watch, and she quickly spread Sudocrem on the affected area. A lovely feeling of relief … ahhhhhhh. A perfect 'baby' moment.

19 AUGUST 2010

Was looking at Jack Redmond's pic on his blog. He is definitely one of those disturbing-looking babies who have the facial characteristics of a man. No turned-up little nose (rather, a genuine 'schnoz'), a 'long' face, oversized ears, and eyebrows almost as bushy as those of a fully-grown adult. I've seen a few of these 'man babies' around, and I don't like the look of them.

22 AUGUST 2010

My baby blog has been making the headlines! Not the front-page headlines – they are firmly fixated on the dreadful economic and political woes of this country – but I still have had a minor brush with fame, via the 'Family Section' in the *Irish Independent*! This featured a rather prominent piece about my baby blog, under the heading, 'Baby Blogger Points Out Ireland's Trials and Tribulations'. Yes, of course the piece was light-hearted and patronising, and high on the 'novelty value' of my writing, but all the same, I couldn't help feeling some pride. Mama and Dada seemed pleased too. Rather predictably, they were featured as 'the proud parents' and, I thought, somewhat to my irritation, they rather exaggerated their own role in encouraging my fledgling career as a political commentator. I sometimes feel that they (and Siobhan Devlin) are really trying to just make money out of all this and cash in on their highly unusual child prodigy. However, none of this could take away from my genuine sense of excitement about seeing my photo in the paper. And I had to admit that I did look really cute!

Bertie
Ahern
ruined my
country

I sum up the mood
of a nation.

23 AUGUST 2010

A convincing piece in *The Irish Times* really does seem to make it abundantly clear that Bertie Ahern ruined my country. Rather like the Devil, and the Wicked Wolf in the Cinderella fairy tale, I can see him becoming a genuine 'hate figure' for babies and young children for generations to come.*

25 AUGUST 2010

Very cynically, having obviously pinched the idea from my baby blog, the *Irish Independent* has published an article by a 2-year-old, who seems to be IN FAVOUR of the bank bailout. It's funny how you get more right-wing as you get older.

---

* Apparently he's also a 'coin jangler' – i.e. someone who enjoys clinking or rubbing coins (usually between three and ten of these, of differing denominations) up against each other in his trouser pockets. Psychologists usually identify this practice as representing a desperate, attention-seeking 'cry for help'. It indicates both an ostentatious display of wealth and, in cases where the coins come in close contact with the testicles, can give the 'jangler' a feeling of intense pleasure.

27 AUGUST 2010

Mama caught Dada looking at 'something he shouldn't be looking at' on the computer. Quite a long-drawn-out, increasingly combative shouting match between parents after they came down from upstairs. (Dada must have been up there for over three hours.) I was genuinely bemused and *very* curious as to what Dada had been up to, but was told I 'wouldn't understand'. I wonder if Dada was looking at cartoons? I can watch about 12 episodes of *Peppa Pig* in a row, even though I don't really know what's going on.

A strange, somewhat intriguing incident. A tiny glimpse of what the adult world is like. DON'T GO THERE!

29 AUGUST 2010

I am getting more and more e-mails and letters in response to my blog. Amazingly, a girl-baby, who was TWENTY MINUTES old, contacted me to express her despair at the state that the country is in. TWENTY MINUTES OLD! And already she fears she is on the scrapheap. It's hard not to feel genuine anger at the politicians.

30 AUGUST 2012

CRAWLING! And not the kind of crawling that the Irish government does to 'our lords and masters' in Europe. This was genuine crawling, across a FLOOR! Over the last few months, I've often thought that I'd like to go from one place to another, but didn't know how to do it. (Rather like the current generation of Irish emigrants hoping to join the workforce in America or Australia, plagued with the daunting prospect of visa and green card applications.) However, yesterday I had the feeling again – a simple, yet overwhelming desire to MOVE! And suddenly it just HAPPENED. I didn't plan a strategy, such as 'Oh, I'm going to put my leg there, and my hand there, and propel myself towards the fireplace'. It was purely instinctive, and soon I felt myself 'moving' slowly across the room, almost in a daze. Probably like an 'out-of-body' experience, but at the same time, a profound 'in-body' experience as well. Dada stumbled across me (literally) as I was edging towards the sofa, and immediately called Mama down from upstairs to witness the 'maiden voyage'! (Sadly, the camcorder purchased specifically to capture such iconic moments needed recharging, and my first independent ramble was lost to posterity.)

Very tired afterwards. (I'd only gone about 5 feet.) Quite an emotional day!

31 AUGUST 2010

We need to ORGANISE! I've noticed that Irish people love to get involved in all kinds of associations and groups – from Tidy Towns' Committees to the Continuity IRA. So why not something for babies too? To this end, had a 'brainstorming' session with Siobhan Devlin this morning, focusing on suggested names for our fledgling pressure group and trying to think up ideas for logos. 'Babies for Changing' was an early name suggestion, but of course that conjures up images of dirty nappies, incontinence, irresponsibility, etc., and so was rejected in favour of 'Babies for Change'. Our logo is simply a photo of me looking angry.

Meanwhile, my joy at learning to crawl has been tempered by seeing Dada produce some kind of 'harness', which I may have to wear in the manner of a dog over the next few years. They obviously want to keep me on a short leash so that I don't run out in front of a car or something. Disappointed by their obvious lack of trust.

3 SEPTEMBER 2010

Aoife Clarke is an enthusiastic member of Babies for Change! She is really 'up for it', and can't wait to get stuck into whatever it is we are going to do (this is a bit unclear at the moment). Jack Redmond was also an early 'joiner-upper'. People can get involved by contacting me via the blog. The only rule is that to join, one has to be under 3 years of age. The 20-minute-old baby is not even our youngest member (because she is now a 'veteran' of almost a week).

We have 50 members already! THRILLED BABY!

An early Babies for Change get-together in Siobhan Devlin's house in Swords.

4 SEPTEMBER 2010

Jack Redmond has left Babies for Change after a 'disagreement on policy and the proposed direction of the organisation'! We hadn't yet decided on our direction, or whether we would even have one! This is MOST annoying. Even worse, *he* has taken 26 members with him and is forming his own pressure group, 'Baby Consensus'. They even have a slogan – 'Heading Forward Together' (very bland, in my opinion). The only thing that could possibly be more irritating than this would be if the organisation's name were in Irish.

5 SEPTEMBER 2010

Baby Consensus has changed its name to '*Páistí*': the Irish for 'babies'. (There is no Irish word for 'consensus'.)

I console myself with the thought that Babies for Change is the second-largest baby activist organisation in the country.

Talked to Siobhan Devlin about the sudden exodus of members, and she is confident that we will reclaim some when the babies in *Páistí* realise that Jack Redmond has no charisma whatsoever, and has a man-baby face.

6 SEPTEMBER 2010

Mentioned on Twitter that Jack Redmond has a man-baby face and my comment got several retweets!

Had a very interesting, informal get-together with some other babies at Siobhan Devlin's house in Swords yesterday evening. Nice to meet some similarly-minded infants. Siobhan Devlin took a picture of some of us sitting on her sofa. We looked like a bunch of very determined youngsters!

7 SEPTEMBER 2010

Fintan O'Toole has signed up for Babies for Change! Sadly though, not the older, well-known polemicist Fintan, but a 3-month-old boy-baby from Cabinteely. However, an accompanying note from his parents reveals that he was called after the *real* Fintan O'Toole, so it's the next best thing!

(The real) Fintan is truly my inspiration. He is very much a 'guru figure'. I often imagine him at home, in his modestly furnished front room, squatting like a Buddhist, dressed in flowing robes, thinking deeply – and then coming up with solutions to the problems of our sad, beleaguered country. Increasingly I ask myself, 'what would Fintan do?' And not just about economic and social matters. Last week I was in the bath and felt a 'wee' coming on. Hmm – should I release into the warm water, or wait until bathtime was over and I was once again safely and firmly sheathed in a nappy? It was a particularly 'baby-centric' dilemma. However, I imagined Fintan in a similar situation. Not, of course, considering whether or not he should wee in the bath, but perhaps addressing a similarly perplexing 'adult' problem – for example, while on the way home from the pub after getting 'langered', suddenly feeling the anguish of a full bladder and contemplating whether to hold on until he reached home, or to go for a slash up against a wall, or in a garden. (I, of course, know that Fintan is the type of person who would hang on until he reached the safety of his own bathroom. Sensible, practical – and hygenic. Brian Cowen and Bertie would, of course, pee in a garden.)

Anyway, I have written to Fintan, asking for an official signed photo!

10 SEPTEMBER 2010

A pathetic response to my 'man-baby' taunt about Jack Redmond: his weak riposte on Twitter is to claim that I am 'babyish'. Of course I am! I'm a baby! The point is: I'm

glad I don't have a man-baby face like him.
(Which, incidentally, doesn't make him look
mature – it just makes him look stupid.)

12 SEPTEMBER 2010

We (Siobhan Devlin, Mama, Dada, and me) have been invited onto a radio programme! We are to be interviewed about the blog, which is really making waves! This seems a lot 'bigger' than the 'Family Section' of the *Irish Independent*.

ROCK AND ROLL!

13 SEPTEMBER 2010

Siobhan Devlin is no longer childminding Jack Redmond. His parents have decided to put him in a crèche because it's cheaper. I'm happy. I felt uncomfortable about having Siobhan Devlin in the Jack Redmond camp, so I regard this as a good thing. (I bet he'll pick up loads of infections and colds in the crèche from all the other infants. I can just imagine rivulets of yellowish baby-snot streaming down his man-baby face.)

14 SEPTEMBER 2010

The radio interview, to my slight disappointment, is not for a national broadcaster, but for a tiny outfit in Bray. I'm still looking forward to it, though.

Coincidentally, the whole country is talking about An Taoiseach Baby-Face Cowen's appearance on the radio (not sure how one can 'appear' on the radio) this morning. He seemed 'sluggish', and the impression given was that he'd been up rather late (after 9 p.m.) the night before. He had allegedly been singing very loudly at a bunch of Fianna Fáilers. On *Morning Ireland** (depressing programme), he was pronouncing his words like a 2-year-old and has been attracting criticism for 'drinking/ carousing', when he should be 'not drinking/ carousing'. Looks like the game could be up for Baby-Face!

---

* Must write to RTÉ and suggest *Morning Ireland* change its name to *Morning! Ireland!* (Much cheerier.)

15 SEPTEMBER 2010

Oh dear. An equally unhappy radio experience for Yours Truly on the Bray radio station, which made me cry. (There was also an air of 'going to the seaside' about the day, which Mama and Dada played up to the hilt, pointlessly pushing me up and down the Bray promenade in my buggy, and buying ice cream cones – for themselves. I believe this is what is called 'forced jollity', and I didn't like it one little bit.)

The radio interviewer was typical of the moronic idiots whose voices I have to listen to every day, blaring out of the radio in Mama's kitchen. He was laughing his head off at the 'novelty' of it all, in a sinister and creepy fashion. I got the impression that he believed that my blog was all the work of Siobhan Devlin (who also appeared on the show to 'channel' me of course), and that I had little or nothing to do with it. I wonder if this is what other people are thinking too? The whole thing was a 'big joke' to this idiot, and he didn't take anything I said seriously.

Afterwards we went to the pub, and Dada began acting as if it was some kind of celebration! After a few drinks were taken (Dada – four pints of lager; Mama – three glasses of wine; Siobhan Devlin – four vodka and tonics), the atmosphere chilled and there was a ferocious argument about 'expenses'. Mama accused Siobhan Devlin of 'unscrupulous behaviour'. It was all very odd and I was quite pissed off, actually.

20 SEPTEMBER 2010

I now have over a thousand followers on Twitter. Most of them are babies, but there are also some surprise names: Spurs and Ireland striker, Robbie Keane and Mary Lou McDonald from Sinn Féin.

21 SEPTEMBER 2010

Discussed with Siobhan Devlin the idea of asking Fintan O'Toole to join Babies for Change. 'He's not a baby,' she said, almost immediately. 'Yes, I know that,' I responded, 'but maybe he might become an honorary member.' I could immediately see the alarm bells going off in Siobhan Devlin's head (literally).

She explained to me that the Nazi Party in Germany was originally a centre-right party composed mostly of mild-mannered people like George Lee and Leo Varadkar, until they let Hitler in and then all hell broke loose. Fintan could have the same effect on Babies for Change.

'Yes,' I retorted, 'but Hitler wasn't an honorary member of the Nazi Party, he was the Fuehrer [Taoiseach].' However, there was no shifting Siobhan Devlin, who was dead against the idea. I suspect there was a 'money' issue here. (There usually is with Siobhan Devlin.)

I ended up throwing my toys out of the pram and screaming, but Siobhan Devlin managed to manipulate the situation, by turning up the radio very loud and putting all my toys in the sink (where I couldn't see them). This confused me, and I eventually got bored and stopped screaming.

Fintan O'Toole will not be joining Babies for Change.

22 SEPTEMBER 2010

I am to do another radio interview, this time with John Murray on his show on RTÉ 1. Siobhan Devlin tells me this is VERY prestigious, so, although I'm a little reluctant after my miserable experience in Bray, which I felt was a bit of a fiasco, I'm willing to give it a go.

Meanwhile, I have received in the post a signed photo of Fintan. I was, of course, completely thrilled about this, but Siobhan Devlin, in typical killjoy fashion, was quick to point out that the autograph on the photo looked incredibly rushed. She then suggested, without any evidence whatever, that maybe Fintan hadn't signed it himself.

I was at first reluctant to accept this, but maybe – just maybe – she's right. The 'autograph' was really just a line scrawled under Fintan's nose, without any kind of attempt to make an even barely legible 'F' or 'OT'. If anything, it looked like a slightly wonky Salvador Dali moustache. It was shoddy work indeed, indicative of the kind of lazy unprofessionalism which Fintan regularly rails against in his newspaper columns. I imagine the great man gets about 50,000–60,000 letters a day (and presumably millions of e-mails), so perhaps, like Elvis Presley, he has some kind of 'Memphis Mafia' army of acolytes around him who pander to his every whim – which would include having them sign 'his' autograph for fans. Realistically, because of his constant campaigning,

Fintan couldn't possibly have the time to do something as trivial as writing his name on a glossy photo.

I still love him, though.

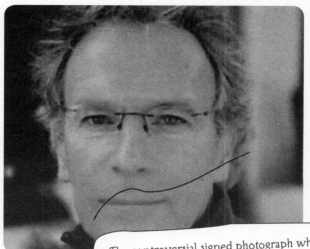

The controversial signed photograph which I received from 'Fintan O'Toole'. Childminder Siobhan Devlin drew my attention to the hastily scrawled and illegible 'autograph'. We immediately suspected foul play.

25 SEPTEMBER 2010

The John Murray Show was a big success! Siobhan Devlin channelled my thoughts magnificently throughout, making me appear articulate and well-informed. Admittedly, at first there was an element of 'the performing seal' about it*, but Murray soon realised that I am very sincere about my beliefs and the conversation eventually reached a level of seriousness and debate about economic matters which must have truly impressed the casual listener. Lots of phone calls to the programme, congratulating me, to the effect of 'we'd-be-better-off-with-that-toddler-running-the-country-than-that-bunch-of-useless-chancers-up-there-in-Dáil-Éireann'. Hear! Hear!

26 SEPTEMBER 2010

Would I really make a better Taoiseach than Baby-Face Cowen? People genuinely seem to feel that I wouldn't do any worse. I played a great game today, where I put

---

* But a *good* element. Like, if you heard a performing seal on the radio and thought, 'That's great'.

together a 'fantasy Emergency Baby Government' featuring lots of my toys.

I thought Charlie, my brown teddy bear, would make a great Tánaiste, and possibly Minister for Foreign Affairs. I handed my dear and loyal old friend, White Teddy, the Finance portfolio. (I felt like Charlie Haughey or Bertie, rewarding their old cronies for blind, unthinking loyalty!) White Teddy has got the necessary presence (mostly a kind of dignified 'stillness') for dealing with frightening, bearded trade union officials, if a time comes when I deem it necessary, for the good of the country, to dismantle the Croke Park Agreement.

Dog Bag, who isn't even a proper toy, but a wash-bag thing with a photo of a dog on it, would be my choice for Minister for the Environment. Gerald, a wooden sheep, would be a great Minister for Agriculture, Fisheries and Food. I must have a 'woman' in my Cabinet, so my choice for Minister for Children and Youth Affairs* would be Dilly, a weird-looking toy, which I think is supposed to be some kind of animal, but I'm honestly not sure. She makes a buzzing sound when I press her tummy, which, for some instinctive reason, I find hilarious. I like the idea of a 'noisy' woman around the table! (Joan Burton springs to mind!!**)

'Aeroplane', as the name implies, is a toy aeroplane which says 'All Aboard' when I fiddle with the propeller, and is the obvious choice for Minister for Transport, Tourism and Sport. I had a long ponder over who I'd like as Minister for Jobs, Enterprise and Innovation, before deciding on Raggles, a really bedraggled-looking homemade

---

* This special 'Ministry for Children' was my own idea. To my disgust, it would be copied (shamelessly) by the new coalition government in March 2011. Also, apparently, there was a 'Ministry for Children and Youth Affairs' under Fianna Fáil, but it was pretty much an 'undercover' outfit which nobody knew anything about, and they never answered the phone.
** Dada now refers to Dilly as 'Joan Burton'!! However, I will not tolerate a maverick spirit and a disloyalty to Cabinet colleagues from Dilly.

teddy (unwanted present from a stingy aunt), who is really just a stuffed sock with canvas ears stuck on the sides.

I'm not sure if I can confer a ministerial portfolio on a ten-piece jigsaw depicting squirrels picnicking, but if I could, I'd like it to take on the demanding Communications, Energy and Natural Resources job. Minister for Arts, Heritage and the Gaeltacht has to go to Ra-Ra (I'm as yet unable to pronounce the word 'rabbit'). A particularly fluffy, cuddly toy who, when I press its tail, makes a noise which sounds a bit like the noise people make when they speak Irish.

After an afternoon of intense negotiations (mostly with myself), I announced the line-up for my newly-formed Cabinet on my blog. I received 20 comments from readers before the day was out, all uniformly agreeing that my collection of toys would do a better job than the current incumbents. Encouraging.

27 SEPTEMBER 2010

Had my first Cabinet meeting of the 'Team Of All Talents'. Nothing much was said, except when I pressed the tummy of Dilly (Children and Youth Affairs) and she emitted her familiar buzzing sound. Aeroplane (Transport, Tourism and Sport) also predictably piped up with 'All Aboard!', which I found summed up the general mood of steely determination around the table. Everyone seemed focused and ready for the difficult tasks which now lie ahead.

30 SEPTEMBER 2010

A poll in the *Evening Herald* asking people who they'd most like to be Taoiseach has given the following result:
1. Enda Kenny
2. Bill Cullen
3. Brian O'Driscoll
4. Jedward
5. Gay Byrne
6. Me!

I think Jedward can be immediately disqualified as a genuine candidate, as you can't have two people as Taoiseach – which means I am bumped up to fifth choice. Yippee!

1 OCTOBER 2010

Made a pretend-Dáil today out of Lego, and filled the seats not occupied by my Cabinet members with Fisher Price Little People figures. It was very impressive! My 'government' even passed some legislation! From now on, corrupt bankers and dodgy developers who don't pay back what they owe will have to sit in a special chair and have brightly-coloured gunge poured over them! Ha, ha!

Later, during the 'afternoon session' (after my sleep), we were having a very lively debate on 'The Banking Crisis' when I accidentally nudged Aeroplane, and he flew off into the Opposition benches, scattering the Little People like skittles! It was almost as undignified as some of the scenes you'd see in the 'real' Dáil.

Oh … if only it wasn't just pretend, and I was really An Taoiseach, with my own hand-picked Cabinet!

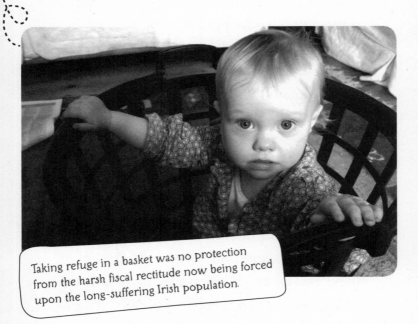

Taking refuge in a basket was no protection from the harsh fiscal rectitude now being forced upon the long-suffering Irish population.

2 OCTOBER 2010

TEETHING! TEETHING! TEETHING! It finally happened! Much worse than my 'phantom' teething of earlier in the year. This is PAINFUL. Mama suspected I might have been 'showboating' a bit, but the tantrum was, for once, justified. Another milestone reached. I reckon I have only another six stages to go before puberty.

4 OCTOBER 2010

I had a huge cry yesterday, as I was feeling very emotional (and still teething a bit). I now feel an increasing burden of expectation on these very young shoulders. A columnist in *The Sunday Times* (Irish edition) described me as 'the Tiny People's Princess'. (Presumably, it's me that's tiny, not the 'People'.) As Bob Dylan said, 'The times they are a-changin.' (Presumably he meant, 'The times are changing'.) I feel that I am on the cusp of greatness.

5 OCTOBER 2010

There is now talk of a 'book deal'. With Siobhan Devlin, I met some publisher-type people. Siobhan Devlin seems to be fully in charge of my 'career' now, to the exclusion of Mama and Dada. I wonder why that is? It could be simply because Siobhan Devlin is a 'big personality'* and Mama and Dada are rather 'wimp-like' and unimpressive.** 'The book' will be about the economy. This type of thing is a 'big seller', and I will be 'up there' with David McWilliams, Shane Ross, Matt Cooper and my beloved Fintan. (I plan to give him a big acknowledgment in my Introduction!)

6 OCTOBER 2010

I seem to be increasingly linked with Jedward in newspaper and magazine articles, as a figure of fun or a 'novelty'

---

* Like Robert Mugabe or Nelson Mandela.

** Like Seán Haughey or Martin Mansergh.

not to be taken seriously.* Siobhan Devlin assures me that the more I get my message 'out there', the more I'll be accepted for the sincere and concerned social, economic and political commentator that I am.

7 OCTOBER 2010

Dada brought home loads of colourful balloons today, and when I accidentally sat on one, it exploded and I was frightened.

10 OCTOBER 2010

I have a 'book deal'!! (At first I was confused, because I thought this might be something like a 'meal deal' in McDonald's or Burger King, but it's not at all similar.) What happened was that yesterday, myself, Siobhan Devlin and Mama met the 'head honchos' of three different book companies, which are called 'publishers'.

---

* Mama said the same thing occurred with Hitler (and, indeed, Mattie McGrath), and, 'look what happened there!'

It was all very exciting. The first lady was very fat and seemed to think that I would be happy to be paid in cuddly toys! Her naïveté was almost touching. So a big 'no' to her, and then on to meet a very important man who lived in a big office. Being a man, his tone was predictably patronising, and he actually proposed that the book would be a POP-UP book, AIMED AT CHILDREN! No thanks!

We 'struck gold' with the third publisher, Gemma Prendergast, someone who at last took us seriously. Yes, obviously I'm not blind to the fact that there is a certain novelty value attached to a baby writing a book on Ireland's economic plight, but that should not obscure the fact that the child in question (me) offers a clear-sighted and unique view of our poor country's immense difficulties. The deal was done for what Siobhan Devlin described as a 'healthy' sum, and we celebrated later with crisps and chocolate!*

15 OCTOBER 2010

I thought a book would consist of about 100 words (like most of my books, such as *Harry the Happy Donkey*), but Siobhan Devlin told me that this deal means I will have to write something with at least 100,000 words! I didn't think there even WERE 100,000 words, but Siobhan Devlin said not to worry – that I could use a lot of the words more than once. But that's still a hell of a lot of work. Luckily, Siobhan Devlin will, of course, be doing the typing. I'll just be 'sounding off', and she will write down what I say. I'm quite looking forward to it. I have A LOT OF THINGS TO GET OFF MY CHEST!

---

* Previously banned – see entry for 2 July – and for good reason. I was hideously sick!

18 OCTOBER 2010

The deadline for the book is, to use a publishing phrase, 'ridiculously tight'. I have to complete it within a few weeks, as well as doing my blog and feeding out bland observations and reflections on my everyday life (and indeed life in general) on Twitter. I will have to cut out my mid-morning sleep, and make do with two hours in the afternoon (as well as my normal twelve hours in the evening, of course). When time is also put aside for playing, nappy changing, feeding, being sick, grumpiness, irritability and petulance, this barely leaves me with an hour for writing each day. For a cut of the fee, Siobhan Devlin has offered to 'ghostwrite' parts of it for me. She is kind of doing this anyway, as I am unable to type, but this will mean that some of 'my' ideas will be originating from Siobhan Devlin. I have little choice but to go along with the idea. There seems to be no other way to get the book out on the shelves for the lucrative 'me' market.

Preparing for another busy day at my desk. (Amateur, out-of-focus pic by Siobhan Devlin.)

NO! NO! NO! NO! NO!

Gemma Prendergast has sent out the press release for the book and it is **SO WRONG!** I thought she understood where I was coming from, but this has got 'novelty book' written all over it:

'Bertie Ahern Ruined My Country: A Toddler's View of Ireland's Economic Crisis
by Katie Woods

All the economists and political commentators have had their say on Ireland's economic troubles, but what about the country's children? In this loveable book, Katie Woods describes what it's like to live in modern-day Ireland from a toddler's perspective, with the belt of austerity tightening more and more around us all every day. Will she have to cut back on cuddly toys and soothers? How can she understand the complexities of **NAMA** and the bank bailout, when she can't even count to two? Katie explores these and other issues in her hilarious debut offering.'

BULLSHIT!

23 OCTOBER 2010

Still very angry about the press release. Luckily, after an urgent phone call from Siobhan Devlin, Gemma Prendergast has agreed to 'put it on hold'. Thank God for that. 'Hilarious debut offering'? No!! My book is a serious work of economic analysis. Siobhan Devlin has explained to me that the PR people have got the wrong end of the stick 'as usual', but that it's a tricky one for them to deal with. I am a 'unique product' and there is no precedent for marketing someone like me. 'Shirley Temple crossed with David McWilliams' has been mentioned. Crass!

'BABIES FOR CHANGE'

Membership Number...1...

Name...Katie Woods...

My Babies for Change membership card!

24 OCTOBER 2010

The first sign of interest from outside Ireland. I (or rather Siobhan Devlin) did a short phone-in with the BBC's Radio 5 live (News and Sport) this morning. I had to content myself with gurgling in the background. (Afterwards, Siobhan Devlin enquired about an 'appearance fee'. She does seem overly money-oriented sometimes.)

25 OCTOBER 2010

Feedback on the BBC website about my spot on the show yesterday. One comment: 'Another sad example of the BBC dumbing down'. Ugh!

30 OCTOBER 2010

Fintan O'Toole, Shane Ross and David McWilliams are heading out 'on tour' around the country, bringing their message of common sense to the voters. Sounds great – a bit like a big Nazi rally, but with middle-aged economists/analysts instead of Nazis. After hearing about it, Siobhan Devlin said to me, 'You should be on that.' Yes, of course I should.

31 OCTOBER 2010

Not a moment to lose! Siobhan Devlin has been on to the promoter of the O'Toole, Ross and McWilliams tour to try and get me 'on board'. Yes, they are all doing impressive work highlighting the incompetence of our bankers and politicians, but it cannot be disguised that they are all white, middle-aged males, representative of only a tiny minority (about 1 per cent) of Irish people. Meanwhile, I am female (50 per cent of Irish people), and young (51 per cent of Irish people). When one adds these figures together, it means that I am representative of 101 per cent of the Irish people. Even Éamon 'Dev' de Valera couldn't have matched that.

2 NOVEMBER 2010

INTENSE negotiations are continuing with the promoter of the 'Big Three' tour. (Will it eventually become the 'Big Four' tour?)

I think Mama and Dada are becoming a little jealous of Siobhan Devlin. She obviously has a lot of 'oomph' that they just don't have, and that is why, in effect, she has become my manager. I LOVE HER!

3 NOVEMBER 2010

I mean, I love Mama and Dada too, but they just don't have any 'oomph', which is badly needed at the moment, for my promotional push. I have plenty of 'oomph' – which must mean 'oomph' isn't hereditary.

4 NOVEMBER 2010

Very disappointing news. Fintan O'Toole is 'dead against' me joining the 'Big Three' on their 'Stick-It-To-The-Bankers/What-The-Hell-Are-We-Going-To-Do-To-Get-Us-Out-Of-This-Mess?' tour of the country. Fintan feels it would 'undermine' his (and Ross's and McWilliams's) credibility. I am crying with sadness.

5 NOVEMBER 2010

I woke up in the middle of the night, screeching at the top of my voice and pondering the idea that possibly I could be the 'support act' on the tour, perhaps appealing to the younger audience who may (wrongly, of course) see Messrs O'Toole, Ross and McWilliams as stuffy old-timers. (I've also heard that Ross threatened to walk off the tour if I was included on the bill. His credibility is now in tatters.)

Mama came in and gave me some Calpol. I felt better immediately. If only our country's economic difficulties could be so easily cured.

6 NOVEMBER 2010

News came back from Siobhan Devlin that McWilliams too was against my 'support act' idea. He still sees himself as very much appealing to young people (fair enough), and prides himself in his ability to 'sex up' economics (fair enough again). I've heard that McWilliams can really 'work' an audience, and at an outdoor gig in Cork hypnotised a horse. He has the charisma of Frank Sinatra mixed with the intellectual ability of Socrates (the philosopher, not the footballer) and frankly, I just can't compete with that. The guy's an A-lister and I'm a Blister. Yes, I am a mixture of youth and experience, but it's 99 per cent youth and 1 per cent experience.

Looks like I'm off the tour before I even got on the bus. VERY DISAPPOINTED BABY!

7 NOVEMBER 2010

Fintan O'Toole (not the baby) has sent me an explanatory note, detailing his concerns about having me on the tour. Of course, as Fintan is still very much my inspiration and mentor, I understand completely. I now realise that it would be like the Rolling Stones going on tour with Justin Bieber. F. also says that he thinks I am doing very good work, and that 'my time will come'. How could I ever have been angry with him? He is so more experienced and wiser than little me. (And arguably cuter – with more abundant hair.) I have asked Siobhan Devlin to somehow obtain a lock of Fintan's wavy mop. I shall take it into my cot with me at night-time. He has a definite teddy bear-like quality. I want to cuddle him!

My message to the bankers and politicians: 'Get Real'.

10 NOVEMBER 2010

The 'Big Time' truly beckons! I am to appear on *The Late Late Show*. Wow!

12 NOVEMBER 2010

I have a child-like disease (literally) called 'croup', which means I bark like a seal. Quite fun! Hope it doesn't stop me going on the *Late Late*, though.

13 NOVEMBER 2010

What would you get if you combined the *Late, Late Show* with *Later ... with Jools Holland*? You'd get the *Late, Late, Later Show with Jools Holland* (and Ryan Tubridy)! This is my first joke!

14 NOVEMBER 2010

Was very nervous before my appearance on the *Late Late*. Threw up very dramatically in the green room over some members of a boy band I'd never heard of before (and never will again). Siobhan Devlin and Dada and Mama were with me. (Sensed some discomfort about this on Siobhan Devlin's part. Luckily, M. and D. didn't appear 'onscreen', as they are both incredibly 'un-telegenic'.) I was third guest on after a prison governor (immensely boring) and forgettable boy band. (Embarrassingly, I also* needed a last-minute nappy change before rushing on!)

Ryan Tubridy was gentle and kind, and only slightly patronising. Like EVERYBODY on television HE IS SMALLER IN REAL LIFE! He tickled me under chin, producing automatic reaction of a smile on my part, which in turn resulted in an automatic cutesy 'ahhh' sound in the audience. Also, Siobhan Devlin said I should have had White Teddy with me, as this would have also helped the image. Hmm. This isn't how I 'see myself' AT ALL, but Siobhan

---

* This 'also' does not refer to the boy band.

Devlin is always banging on about 'good market positioning', etc. Hmm. But at least we managed to plug the book ('out first thing in the New Year' – thanks, Ryan!), and were back in the green room in time to see Daniel O'Donnell on the TV screen warbling about the green fields of Donegal. (I hate him.*)

I have done it! I have done *The Late Late Show*! An immense sense of achievement.

HAPPY BABY!

15 NOVEMBER 2010

WILL THERE BE A BAILOUT?** Denials from the government! Noel Dempsey and Dermot Ahern*** say 'no'! What's happening?! The media awash with speculation. As I was glued to the radio, listening to all of this, Siobhan Devlin presented me with what

---

* So does White Teddy.

** Yes.

*** Fianna Fáilers. An unconvincing double act, like Pinky and Perky.

she described as a 'very exciting proposal'. She has urged me to sign up with a company called 'Brand Strategy Ireland'.

This from their website: 'Brand Strategy Ireland delivers successful social media strategies. We use Facebook, Twitter and LinkedIn to target *your* market, to achieve a successful client-based single-channel solution platform, which provides maximum national and international multi-channel exposure.'

This is all marketing gobbledygook to me, but Siobhan is insistent that I sign up with them.

OK!

16 NOVEMBER 2010

The bailout from Europe, which they swore wasn't going to happen, has happened. This, in essence, means we're f***ed. I will spend the rest of my life working to pay back those faceless bureaucrats. AM FUMING!

Meanwhile, no sooner had I signed up with Brand Strategy Ireland than I noticed this on their website: 'Our expertise and professional campaigns are already working for some of the world's biggest names, such as: Coca-Cola, O2, Shell and Adidas, along with well-known Irish brands like Unislim, Dunnes Stores, Horse Racing Ireland and Katie Woods.'

I am a 'brand'!!

22 NOVEMBER 2010

Discussed the possibility of a future book signing in Easons in O'Connell Street with Siobhan Devlin and Gemma Prendergast, until we all remembered that I can't write. Gemma suggested a 'palm print' in poster paint instead. Why not?!

The Greens are pulling out of government! I thought this was peculiar, as I presumed 'The Greens' were a family. Apparently not. They are a political party who wear beards, eat veggie food, and drink milk for pleasure. I can't say I'll miss them, as I didn't even know they were there!

23 NOVEMBER 2010

Ireland has definitely gone bust. After denying that there was any need for it, the government went cap in hand to the IMF and asked for loads of cash! Oh, so frustrating that I can't do anything about it except scream.

The Germans: Fiscal rectitude imposed from Europe could be a threat to Ireland's sovereignty.

AHHHH HHH HH HHH HH HHHH HHH H HHH
HH HH HHHHH HHH HHH HH HHH HHHH H HHH!!

A black day for the country, as we
hand over our sovereignty to a bunch of
foreigners.

ENRAGED BABY!

24 NOVEMBER 2010

A family break in a hotel in Wicklow.
(Mama got some 'deal'.) I was given the
distinct impression, as we were driving
down in the car, that Mama and Dada
don't like Siobhan Devlin. The word
'shifty' was used. Then, the next day, I
heard Dada remark over breakfast, while
I was struggling with pushing a small
piece of toast down my throat, '*We* made
her, you know.' I was a bit confused by
this. How did they in some way 'make'
me? Didn't I just suddenly and somewhat
mysteriously arrive, attached by a sling to
the beak of a stork, like every other baby

in the world? (Must google 'childbirth' to confirm this.) Very strange. I think they're jealous, because Siobhan Devlin has been so successful in promoting me as one of Ireland's leading political and economic commentators (admittedly, with some novelty value thrown in).

25 NOVEMBER 2010

Good news! The economic situation is so dire that Jack Redmond's parents (and Jack) have been forced to leave the country, so that his father can look for gainful employment in England. (Apparently they bought their house, little more than the size of a shoebox, for €1.2 million in 2006. It's now on the market for 50 grand). As my star ascends, his ridiculous *Páistí* organisation will become less and less relevant. Hit the road, Jack! You contributed NOTHING to this country, and now you're going to grow up with an accent like Ken Livingstone!

26 NOVEMBER 2010

Hmm ... I think I was a little harsh on little Jack, there. Another spell of uncomfortable teething may have made me a little irritable. I have sent out 'feelers' to the remaining members of *Páistí* (12 infants aged from 3 to 18 months) asking them to re-join Babies for Change. It all feels like a mini version of the Northern Ireland Peace Process. However, the reality of the situation (I feel like Martin McGuinness now) is that Babies for Change is now the only show in town, and it's time for tiny tots to present a united front.

27 NOVEMBER 2010

Siobhan Devlin brought me over to Aoife Clarke's for a play around. I like Aoife! She looks strangely older, and, I must say, somewhat in need of a haircut. We threw plastic bricks at each other, then did some 'rough housing' outside, resulting in a grazed knee for the youngest of the Clarke litter. 'A Grazed Knee' – one of the great childhood clichés, and also a good title for a book.

I sometimes get the feeling that Aoife Clarke doesn't like Siobhan Devlin. Or maybe she doesn't trust her? Something's not quite right …

Writing a stern letter to *The Irish Times* – in crayon.

Pretty illegible, as at this point I was still unable to write. (Still can't!) But the strong crayon marks show my righteous anger.

28 NOVEMBER 2010

I'd really love to go on tour, preaching my baby common sense all over Ireland. Siobhan Devlin would of course be my road manager, and I'd take Aoife Clarke along for company. Discussed the idea with Siobhan Devlin, who sniffed another money-making opportunity. 'We must strike while the iron is hot!' (Not sure what this means – Siobhan Devlin likes saying it. I am usually discouraged from being around hot irons.)

30 NOVEMBER 2010

Siobhan Devlin has been contacting various promoters, and the best she has

MCO Promotions presents

THE REMAINS OF ST THÉRÈSE OF LISEUX

The souvenir brochure for my Irish tour supporting the remains of St Thérèse of Lisieux.

Plus support: child blogger/activist: *katy WOODS*

IRISH TOUR 2010

Dec 16 - Ferns (Arts Centre)
Dec 17 - Moate (Community Hall)
Dec 18 - Monaghan (Dessie O'Hare Centre)
Dec 19 - Loughrea (Tent near town)
Dec 20 - Limerick Prison

been able to do is get me a support slot for the remains of St Thérèse of Lisieux, which are going on a tour of Ireland next week. (Despite being dead, St Thérèse attracts a huge, enthusiastic live following around the country, as if she were the Beatles or something.) Apparently, another relic has pulled out, so there is a vacancy. Basically, in various venues around the country, I would do a five-minute talk before the remains go on display. But is this my audience? Siobhan Devlin is keen for me to do it.

1 DECEMBER 2010

Another December … Hang on! This is the first December I remember, so I shouldn't have said 'another'.

Cold.

Hiccups.

Loud burping.

15 DECEMBER 2010

Accompanied by my minder/tour manager Siobhan Devlin and child companion Aoife Clarke, I am about to go on tour around Ireland with the remains of St Thérèse of Lisieux.

16 DECEMBER 2010

Ferns. On tour with the remains of St Thérèse of Lisieux. It's snowing. I love the snow.

17 DECEMBER 2010

Moate. On tour with the remains of St Thérèse of Lisieux. More snow.

18 DECEMBER 2010

Monaghan. On tour with the remains of St Thérèse of Lisieux. Snowy.

19 DECEMBER 2010

Loughrea. On tour with the remains of St Thérèse of Lisieux. Lots of snow. Perhaps too much?

20 DECEMBER 2010

Limerick Prison. On tour with the remains of St Thérèse of Lisieux. Enough of this snow!

21 DECEMBER 2010

'Dem Bones! Dem Bones!' *Thank Christ* that's over. What a freak show! It was **AWFUL!** I have never been so bored (or cold) in my life. The punters were only interested in the remains of St Thérèse, and hardly anybody came to hear my interesting talks on the economy (complete with slide show or, as Siobhan Devlin calls it, 'fully interactive multimedia display'). What a disaster! My name was misspelt in the shoddy-looking souvenir programme, alongside a photo of me downloaded from the internet, looking particularly baby-like.* After paying Siobhan Devlin and Aoife Clarke, I have barely made €60. And

---

* I was wearing a salad bowl on my head, placed there by Dada, in a failed attempt to make me look 'playful'.

it was totally the 'wrong' audience – mostly ladies in their eighties (some genuine 'old crones' complete with scary black shawls!). Appearing in a bloomin' pantomime with Jedward would have been a much better idea!

ANGRY AND ANNOYED BABY!!

22 DECEMBER 2010

I have had an offer to appear in pantomime with Jedward (along with White Teddy – apparently he's now some kind of cult figure, after his appearance alongside me on *The Late Late Show*). I was wary at first, fearing that they wanted me to appear as the baby Jesus in a nativity scene or something, but I've been assured that my 'public image' (I am, after all, a 'brand') won't be disrespected or ridiculed. As part of a dream sequence in the panto, I will be 'interviewed' on stage by an actor playing Fintan O'Toole (but dressed as a giant fairy). I'm receiving the script later today. Hopefully it won't be too light-hearted or trivial.

23 DECEMBER 2010

Boy, was I wrong about that. **THE WHOLE SCRIPT IS LIGHT-HEARTED AND TRIVIAL!** There is hardly any serious analysis of the economic state of the country at all. I would have expected a little more gravitas and solemnity in a vehicle which is to feature the talents of Jedward. Against the wishes of Siobhan Devlin, I have turned down the role.*

24 DECEMBER 2010

This morning, Dada, rather against my will, forced me to open a window on the advent calendar with my chubby fingers. A pointless exercise. What is my reaction supposed to be, when a tiny window is pulled open from the backing paper,

---

* As it turned out, the WRONG decision! The production made €20 million.

revealing a crude depiction of an infant Jesus, a snowman or a Santa figure? Surprise? Delight? Excitement? Rather, the emotion is one of boredom mixed with mild nausea. I get no pleasure from it. Dada shows signs of irritation with me, but I am unable to affect any kind of interest in this dismal and outdated ritual.

I had had a bit of a ding-dong with Siobhan Devlin yesterday, after turning down the Jedward panto role, which has left me in rather a depressed state, so I was in even less of an 'advent calendar' mood. Siobhan Devlin said the panto was 'money for old rope'*, and pointed out that I was 'unlikely to be acted off the stage by Jedward'. But money is surely not the sole reason for doing anything (unless you're Charles J. Haughey)?

---

* See previous * above, re. the financial success of the panto.

25 DECEMBER 2010

I just cannot see the appeal of Christmas for children. Certainly, for babies like me, it's more or less the same as any other day. I wake up at the same time, yell and scream no less nor no more than any other day and am, as yet, unable to enjoy the delights of alcohol. (Dada 'crashed out' at about four in the afternoon, having drunk two bottles

My first Christmas of austerity. I emerge from under a chair and am immediately disappointed by the tiny (and cheap) tree and lack of presents.

of wine, eaten loads of turkey and knocked back an Irish coffee and half a bottle of Baileys.) I did get a present, but it was just another toy – in fancy wrapping paper, for once. *ZZZZZZZZZZZZZZ* ∞

26 DECEMBER 2010

I have 20,001 followers on Twitter and loads of Facebook friends. I am a successful brand. But Siobhan Devlin wants to take me 'to the next level'. With this end in mind, she has suggested that I stand as the official Babies for Change candidate in the next general election. After thinking about it (for no more than ten seconds!), I agreed.

27 DECEMBER 2010

I announced on Twitter that I will be standing (or, as our UK friends would say, I will be 'stood'!) in the next election, and I received several hundred 'you'd-do-a-lot-

better-than-that-shower-up-there-in-Dáil-
Éireann' type replies.

I feel the hand of History on my shoulder.

28 DECEMBER 2010

Should I really say things like, 'I feel the
hand of History on my shoulder'? It's what
loser politicians like Bertie Ahern say, and
it doesn't mean anything. I must be the
candidate who avoids cliché. I must offer
a fresh start to a jaded electorate, and be a
genuine challenger who will give hope to
a generation that feels alienated from the
affairs of Leinster House. I genuinely feel
this is the most important election in my
lifetime.

I am crying.

29 DECEMBER 2010

Just doing a little research on the history
of Irish politics. The secret of success
seems to be to form a political party with a

Down To Business: Me ('An Taoiseach') at the Cabinet table with Minister for Finance, 'Dilly' (on right). Also present are Minister for Social Affairs, 'White Teddy' and Minister for the Environment, 'Dog Bag'.

paramilitary wing, kill loads of people and then arrange some kind of 'peace process', after which you stop killing people and blame the casualties on a 'conflict' where everybody did 'bad things', but no one has to say sorry. People will be so grateful that you're not killing people any more that they'll vote for you in droves. Irish people seem to really **LOVE** this type of thing, and it's a big vote-winner at elections.

Discussed this possible strategy with Siobhan Devlin, but she feels that 'cuteness' is a big selling point of Babies for Change, and that therefore killing people wouldn't be the way to go, even if the dead are subsequently deemed to be part of a 'conflict' that nobody seems to be responsible for. It all seems a bit 'Irish' to me. **CONFUSED BABY!**

Must think of a good, original slogan for my posters, leaflets and so on. A brainstorming session with Siobhan Devlin scheduled for tomorrow, to really get the juices flowing.

30 DECEMBER 2010

A good meeting with Siobhan Devlin. We decided it's important that I put something in my campaign literature about how great Ireland is. The Irish love reading about how brilliant they are, so I intend to mention:

1. We are a proud people.
2. We have an entrepreneurial spirit. (Despite rarely being able to spell 'entrepreneurial'.)
3. We have bright and educated young people. (Despite rarely being able to spell 'entrepreneurial'.)
4. We are creative, loved and respected internationally. (The Irish ESPECIALLY love being told how great we are by foreigners – even better, if they are impressive foreigners like the Yanks.)
5. It is important that we believe in ourselves and we can only do this by working together.
6. This election is about the FUTURE!
7. IRELAND IS OPEN FOR BUSINESS!

31 DECEMBER 2010

On reflection, all those slogans are so clichéd and banal that only a moron could vote for a candidate who came out with such meaningless drivel. Despite protests from Siobhan Devlin that one should never overestimate the intelligence of the Irish electorate, I have thrown all these ideas in the bin. I have literally consigned them to 'the dustbin of History'.

1 JANUARY 2011

While canvassing, am I expected to kiss babies for photo opportunities? That will look weird.

2 JANUARY 2011

Deliberately ignored the fact that it was 1 January yesterday. 'It's time to look forwards, not back.'

3 JANUARY 2011

I've been reading about something called the 'United Left Alliance'. I thought they were a turban-wearing organisation who used to fight the Taliban in the Afghanistan mountains, but no – they're just the latest Irish political party with the word 'left' in their name. (Previous parties include Democratic Left and Turn Left at the Lights.) This current 'Left Alliance' is a group of curiously unattractive and unsmiling people who are not in one political party but have a lot in common with each other (apart from all being unattractive and unsmiling). Should we at Babies for Change throw in our lot with them? I get the impression that this bunch of lefties (literally) are a VERY serious crowd, and that there aren't many laughs to be had at the various meetings they hold in function rooms in pubs and hotels. But, as Siobhan Devlin said to me when I mentioned this, 'If you want a bundle of laughs, join a circus.' (Not actually a great example. Trapeze artists and lion-tamers rarely raise a smile, and, from what I've seen, clowns are just embarrassing.) Still, it's an intriguing proposition: an alliance between the free-thinking liberals of the ULA and the progressive and energetic membership of Babies for Change.

There is an 'event' organised by the ULA in a function room in a hotel tomorrow night. They are no doubt hoping to attract similarly-minded radicals, and I feel I certainly tick that box. I intend to go along with Siobhan Devlin and put out 'feelers' …

5 JANUARY 2011

Arrived at the hotel, and initially went to another function room where a meeting was taking place for survivors of clerical abuse. (The WRONG place to put out 'feelers'.*) When we eventually found the right function room, it became clear that

---

* Although I'm sure many of those present would have been determined to see 'feelers' expelled from the Catholic Church! Ha, ha!

the head honchos of the ULA wanted little to do with Babies for Change. I bumped into several Communists and lesbians (including some Communist lesbians), but it was clear none were willing to engage in meaningful political dialogue.

Me with my toy plastic farm. I look concerned that it may be judged 'a second home', and would thus become eligible for tax.

Siobhan Devlin and I reckon this is because they see the party as childish and naïve (ho-hum!), and our baby members as unable to carry out the basic duties of a fledgling political coalition: e.g. book function rooms in hotels and get rounds of drinks in. I felt the pain of discrimination very strongly, and left* feeling marginalised. At not yet 1 year old, I find myself already disillusioned with the Left**.

6 JANUARY 2011

A worrying thought: there is probably some stipulation about who can become a member of the Dáil, and I am concerned that, as a baby, I may not be able to take my rightful place in parliament. Siobhan Devlin mentioned this to Dada, and he made a rather funny remark: 'Yes, you're right. In order to get into the Dáil you have to be a middle-aged, overweight man – and preferably a member of Fianna Fáil!'

---

* Other meaning of the word.
** Back to original meaning of the word.

Joking aside, it's a serious issue which could have ramifications* for my candidacy. However, Siobhan Devlin reckons that I will pick up a strong 'protest vote' and almost certainly be elected. This could lead to a 'constitutional crisis', if I am deemed – as a result of my age – too young to represent my constituents. A referendum costing several million Euros (most of it pocketed by lawyers) may be required to ensure that I can take my seat in our national parliament. However, becoming a TD is my dream and nobody can put limitations on a dream. (Nice sentiment there! Reminds me of Martin Luther King, Nelson Mandela, Judy Garland, etc.)

7 JANUARY 2011

Not long until my book is published (tomorrow). I will soon be back on the wearying publicity treadmill of radio and television appearances, and (for the first

* Check word.

time) book signings (or rather, 'palm-imprinting' in pink* poster paint).

14 JANUARY 2011

The book is 'out there'! However, I got wildly over-excited at the prospect of being a published (child) author, which resulted in a slight temperature, and I couldn't go to the launch! I was watching *In the Night Garden* with a third-choice (and third-rate) babysitter, while Siobhan Devlin and Mama and Dada and Aoife Clarke had a great time at my party! Mama and Dada stumbled home at about 1.30 in the morning, Dada obviously having enjoyed fully the delights of the free bar. Oh well, at least I'll be fresh for my book signing tour, which begins tomorrow in Athlone.

FRUSTRATED BABY!

---

* Again, must once more stress, regarding 'gender politics' issue: pink nothing to do with female stereotyping – I just like the colour (a lot).

15 JANUARY 2011

Siobhan Devlin is furious that the hotel we're staying in here in Athlone has inadequate crèche facilities. She obviously has a friend in the town (or the surrounding area), whom she wanted to meet up with. 'They've got a freakin' spa and a gym, but no crèche!' she exclaimed loudly to me just before supper. She then ranted and raved about the fact that she couldn't go out, and was plainly unhappy at being forced into the undesirable situation of having to stay in to look after little me. I too have noted the number of hotels in this country which boast of their superb spa and opportunities for all kinds of 'treatments', and their common inducements for 'pampering', etc. Yet one despairs at the lack of crèche facilities. I could possibly make an election pledge to do something about the issue of these facilities generally. There may be 'votes in it' …

I wonder if Siobhan Devlin was meeting a 'man'? She looks to me like a virgin.

16 JANUARY 2011

I'm not really sure what a virgin is. I suppose it's someone who looks like Siobhan Devlin.

20 JANUARY 2011

The book tour has been going well. Lots of people have turned up to get their books imprinted with my tiny pink palm. One notable incident in Ennis: I overturned a pot of pink paint and a batch of Celia Ahern's over-hyped *P.S. I Love You* was destroyed. If only it had been her father's autobiography, instead!

21 JANUARY 2011

Baby-Face has called a general election. It will take place on 25 February! So much to be done. Will need major strategy meeting with Siobhan Devlin.

VERY EXCITED BABY!

22 JANUARY 2011

The word on the street (and in *The Irish Times*) is that Fintan is considering standing for the Dáil! This is great news! At last – one of 'us', who will take on the greedy, immoral, corrupt politicians at their own game.*

While genuinely thrilled that my all-time hero plans to contest the election, at the same time, the thought occurred to me: is my own candidacy a 'dead rubber'? After all, Fintan and I have been literally 'singing from the same hymn sheet' for quite some time. However, Siobhan Devlin was quick to reassure me that there is room for us both on the political spectrum, and that Fintan will possibly 'bottle it' anyway. Was unsure of the meaning of the expression 'bottle it', as I still completely associate the word 'bottle' with babies' bottles. The phrase was eventually explained to me by a

---

* Could be interpreted as implying that Fintan would use greed, immorality and corruption to further his political ambitions. This is not the meaning I intend.

leering Siobhan Devlin, who seemed to be in a particularly cynical and sceptical mood (she was possibly drunk).

ELECTION 2012!!!!

BABIES FOR CHANGE
MANIFESTO

'Sensible Policies For A Nicer Ireland'
***

OUR 7 POINT PROGRAMME FOR PROGRESS:

1. Build more prisons! (Including one especially for bankers.)
2. Ignore The Troika!
3. End austerity!
4. No water or household charges!
5. Everyone in the country to agree to be in bed by seven o'clock. (Less electricity will be used in the evenings, so everything is more efficient!)
6. Introduction of pram lanes (to go alongside cycle lanes.)
7. More playgrounds.

VOTE KATIE WOODS -
YOUR 'BABIES FOR CHANGE' CANDIDATE!**

**Katie not on official list of candidates seeking election However, your spoilt vote will indicate support for 'Babies for Change'.

I remain extremely proud of our 2011 election manifesto, despite the fact that it mistakenly says '2012' instead of 2011.

23 JANUARY 2011

Election fever became somewhat muted when I received a bill for €3,000 from Brand Strategy Ireland! What have they actually **DONE?!** Siobhan Devlin says she's not exactly sure either, but thinks we should pay them anyway, especially with the election coming up. 'Marketing' really does seem to me to be a lot of nappy mess, but I'm assured it's very important in the world of modern media communications.*

24 JANUARY 2011

In all the excitement about the election, I nearly forgot that I have to put together an **ELECTION MANIFESTO!** Very important that I get this right, as voters really love attractive policies. It's crucial that I 'tap into' what the electorate wants, and serve them up a dish of delicious initiatives and solutions for the country's problems. It is **IMPERATIVE** that I

---

* Bollocks.

put a winning proposal together, and give the people just what they want.

Here are the main points ('Our Seven-Point Programme For Progress') which Babies for Change would propose putting in place:

Sensible Policies for a Happier Ireland (great tagline by Siobhan Devlin!)

- Build more prisons! (Including one especially for bankers.)
- Ignore The Troika!
- End austerity!
- No water or household charges!
- Everyone in the country to agree to be in bed by seven o'clock! (Less electricity will be used in the evenings, so everything more efficient.)
- Introduction of pram lanes (to go alongside cycle lanes)!
- More playgrounds!

Yes, some of these proposals are certainly 'baby-centric', but I think that's fine, as the party is of course called Babies for Change. And people generally like babies. I sincerely believe that there is something there for everyone. (Secretly surprised at how easy it is to put together a manifesto which will surely please all the citizens of the country!)

Maddeningly, I noticed too late that 'Election 2012' had been mistakenly printed at the top of the manifesto. This may have lost me several hundred votes, as some people might end up delaying their visit to the polling station for another year.

25 JANUARY 2011

Siobhan Devlin had a look at the manifesto and asked where all the money is going to come from to pay for it all. I looked at her blankly. Higher taxes or something? Luckily, I don't have to worry about that until my first day in government.

26 JANUARY 2011

The Mayor of Portlaoise has asked me back next year to turn on the town's Christmas lights. I overheard him say to Siobhan Devlin afterwards, as they both sipped sherry in the council offices, 'As long as the novelty hasn't worn off.' Not an encouraging caveat. Will there even BE Christmas lights this time next year? (Also, I've heard a strong rumour that Portlaoise may not make it through the next 12 months.) I overheard this remark somewhere recently (possibly from a bus driver): 'Could the last person left in the country please turn off the lights?' A stark reminder of the lack of respect that the ordinary people have for our politicians. It is my task to win back that respect.

28 JANUARY 2011

Resting after arduous, but successful, book imprinting tour. Went to the zoo yesterday with Mama and Dada. Animals are really funny-looking. Saw a picture of three very weird-looking beasts. These, I was informed, were called 'rhinoceroses'. (Or rather, two of them were – the other was Brian Cowen, yawning while opening their new enclosure.)

On the political front, the country is reeling from the news that Fintan is NOT running for the Dáil! This is a BIG DEAL! It's all in this morning's *Irish Times*. Apparently, earlier this year, Fintan was waiting outside the changing rooms in Marks & Spencer, as his son tried on some hats. In less than five minutes, upwards of 600 people approached him and asked him to run in the election. Impressed (and humbled) by this, he decided then and there to literally consider putting his money where his mouth was. 'Well, I'm criticising all these politicians, so I, as an ordinary* member of the public, have a duty to run for public

---

* Not that ordinary.

office and change things from the inside,' he probably thought.*

At the zoo. Even elephants will have to live with the grim consequences of Ireland's reckless economic policies for years to come.

---

* Speculation by me. Actual words used here may not be the same as those formed in Fintan's mind.

But now, sadly, after what looks to me like a major rethink, Fintan has decided that time constraints would not allow himself and other independently-minded individuals to mount a legitimate campaign for reform. It's a BLACK DAY for democracy. However, I feel the mantle (Fintan's mantle) has very much been passed to me, and that I now carry the responsibility of bringing many of my mentor's ideas and initiatives into the heart of Irish public life.

I relish the challenge. (Feel that I should end this entry with a rousing phrase in Irish, but sadly don't know any.)

29 JANUARY 2011

Apparently, at a recent FF Cabinet meeting, Brian Cowen called me a 'ridiculous baby'. Harrumph! HE LOOKS LIKE A RHINOCEROS! (However, during the election campaign, I must resolve not to resort to name-calling.)

31 JANUARY 2011

On the news, I heard a hopeful candidate say that he was 'getting a good reaction from the doorsteps'. Not much use, I'd say, as doorsteps can't vote.

1 FEBRUARY 2011

Ah – it's a good reaction '*on*' the doorsteps! (I obviously misheard.) This still doesn't make sense, but it kind of means (according to Dada) that when candidates call unexpectedly on potential voters in their homes, the resident says that they (i.e. the candidates) are great and are doing a tremendous job. 'Getting a good reaction on the doorsteps' is a useful phrase that politicians employ when talking to 'the media'. Whether anybody really likes the candidate or not doesn't matter: it's just something 'they say'. I'm not much bigger than a doorstep, so I'll need my election team (most likely Siobhan Devlin and Aoife

Clarke) to lift me up, so that my potential supporter can have a good gawk at me. (Actually, Aoife Clarke is barely bigger than a doorstep herself, so it looks like Siobhan Devlin will be doing all the hoisting.)

Am also taking White Teddy with me. I have mentioned his 'stillness' before, and my nominee for Minister for Finance cuts an impressive figure on the hustings. Siobhan Devlin (admittedly after several gin and tonics) has compared him to Générale de Gaulle. I sometimes worry that he might launch a successful bid for the leadership. Then I remember that he is still essentially a fluffy toy.

2 FEBRUARY 2011

Siobhan Devlin thinks that we should get a special election vehicle that I can travel around in while I gauge opinion on the notorious doorsteps. She had an idea that we could call it 'The Battle Buggy'. She reckons we can 'soup up' my current, rather dilapidated buggy and decorate it with stickers, bunting, slogans and other election paraphernalia.

VERY 'UP FOR IT' BABY!

3 FEBRUARY 2011

I'm hoping that I'll be invited to the televised 'Leaders' Debate' to chew over the major issues with Baby-Face and Enda and a few other party heads. I can certainly 'take' Baby-Face, now that the country resembles Germany in the 1920s, but Enda looks like a canny individual, who has his sights firmly set on being the next leader of our proud but bruised country. I'll have to make sure all the 'facts and figures' are at my fingertips before I go into the gladiatorial arena.

4 FEBRUARY 2011

Today I was wheeled around Dundrum Shopping Centre by Siobhan Devlin (with

Babies for Change fundraising 'Bucket-A-Thon' event in Dundrum Shopping Centre.

Aoife Clarke in tow), to 'meet and greet' the ordinary people of Ireland ('ordinary' being a particularly appropriate word to describe them), and attend a 'Baby Bucket-A-Thon' fundraising event. This involved a lot of babies splashing around in buckets, and was actually as weird as it sounds. Overall, though, a successful day of campaigning. I felt I genuinely did get a 'good reaction', if not on the doorsteps then on the hard tiles of the shopping centre.

5 FEBRUARY 2011

A drunken Dada, in expansive mood, leaned over my cot last night and said, 'Wash your back with Siobhan Devlin.' I wasn't entirely sure what he meant. Siobhan Devlin does occasionally wash my back. She did it only last week, when I fell into a muddy puddle while out canvassing. I had to nip into a city-centre hotel for a quick wash. (The hotel manager took a photograph, which can now be viewed in the lobby, alongside other photos of the manager with Patrick Duffy (Bobby Ewing in *Dallas*) and Gabriel Byrne.) Still, it was an odd thing for Dada to say.

6 FEBRUARY 2011

Day 2 on the campaign trail! The festooned-with-stickers-and-bunting Battle Buggy (with me in it) was paraded through Grafton Street, where I was again warmly welcomed by lots of ordinary people. But, lo and behold, fate intervened in a way I could never have expected. As we turned the corner into Nassau Street, we were instantly confronted by the new Fianna Fáil leader* and some of his brawny henchmen. The FF posse was also pounding the pavement, pressing the flesh, and generally trying to pick up votes for their hapless candidate (presumably from people who have been living in caves for the last year, and are unaware of the complete hames their party have made of running the show).

When the new leader saw my cute, innocent little face, presuming me to be a bog-standard infant member of the general public, he immediately saw a photo opportunity and tried to wrench me out of The Battle Buggy so that he could give me a kiss. I must have been recognised by one of his goons, because the new leader was soon informed about who exactly he was trying

---

* Must look up his name.

to co-opt for a photo op – i.e., not a cuddly 'prop', but a high-profile candidate from another party, and one of his sternest critics! I was instantly dropped back into the cot and the FF mob ran off like a bunch of guilty youths who had just thrown a brick through a sweet-shop window. However, there were many media people and photographers present to see the incident, and I am hoping that there may be something about it in tomorrow's paper!

7 FEBRUARY 2011

Hah!

MARTIN'S WALKABOUT BACKFIRES

The new leader of Fianna Fáil, Micheál Martin, found himself in an embarrassing situation yesterday, when a walkabout in Dublin city centre led to a confrontation with one of his political rivals: infant politician, Katie Woods, founder of the Babies for

Change Party. At first the FF chief seemed unaware of the identity of the child, and picked her up, intending to give her a kiss and cuddle in front of the watching press. However, he was quickly informed that the infant has been a stern critic of his party and was unlikely to welcome the attention. Indeed, Woods has political ambitions of her own, and intends to contest a seat in the forthcoming general election. The under-fire Fianna Fáil supremo immediately dropped the screaming child back in her buggy (currently referred to as 'The Battle Buggy' for the duration of her election campaign), and hastily made his way up Grafton Street in search of less critical voters.'

I wouldn't have used the word 'screaming' ('indignant moaning' might have been nearer the mark), but everything else was extremely accurate. Great publicity, and still only Day 2!

8 FEBRUARY 2011

Irony piles upon irony. Mama and Dada received a letter this morning from the 'former Taoiseach' Bertie Ahern, asking them to vote for the new leader. I noticed his facsimiled signature under a self-congratulatory list (noticeably short) of his achievements as Taoiseach, including of course, the 'Peace Process', which he is always banging on about. This, according to Dada, was just a complete capitulation to the IRA, 'like the Allies surrendering to Hitler in 1945 – a 2-year-old child could have negotiated that'. Indeed.

The former Taoiseach's missive was crumpled up and despatched to the bin in double-quick time, from whence it was later retrieved and 'pooped on' by a dog.

9 FEBRUARY 2011

Siobhan Devlin has been on to RTÉ about having me (and her, as she'd have to 'translate') on the Party Leaders' televised debate. They (actually, a 19-year-old dogsbody called Orla) hummed and hawed about it, saying things like 'Well, it'll be past her bedtime' and (bizarrely), 'She'll need milk'! Looks like they won't allow me on.

In all the flurry of electioneering, I almost forgot it was my birthday! Some small treats received – a milkshake and a book about colours (boring).

11 FEBRUARY 2011

Hmm … There is a flaw in my plan to run for election to the Dáil. Siobhan Devlin checked the Citizens Information website, and it states that a candidate has to be at least 21 years of age to run for election. That leaves me about 240 months short of the required criterion. However, both Siobhan Devlin and I (and Mama and Dada) think that I should put myself forward as an unofficial candidate and target the voters

Mama (mostly out of picture) tries to interest me in some shapes. I was more interested in the 'shape' of the Irish economy.

who usually choose to spoil their vote. By voting for me, an Independent candidate not on the official list, they will still be spoiling their vote, but spoiling it in a more constructive way. Another advantage is that, by not running in any specific constituency, I can stand in EVERY constituency (kind of). Was thinking up slogans last night for this strategy: 'Every Spoilt Vote is a Vote for Babies for Change'. Will try to set up a meeting with Brand Strategy Ireland to see what they think is the best way forward to develop this plan.

12 FEBRUARY 2011
Brand Strategy Ireland not returning any of Siobhan Devlin's calls, nor responding to her e-mails.

13 FEBRUARY 2011
Brand Strategy Ireland have gone out of business. They have debts of €500,000, and their CEO has fled to South America. Beginning to think that paying them €3,000 last month (on the advice of Siobhan Devlin!) may not have been a good idea.

14 FEBRUARY 2011
While on election walkabout today, an ordinary member of the public, on having

one of my 'Vote for Me!' leaflets proffered to her, replied, in a somewhat sneering tone, 'You politicians are all the same.' I'm plainly not the same!* I'm a baby, for goodness' sake! Can't people tell the difference? Just goes to show how cynical the general populace have become.

Later, I watched the Leaders' Debate on RTÉ, from which I was BARRED. All very boring. Just a lot of white, middle-aged men in suits. I was hoping that Gerry Adams might have worn his paramilitary gear, just so he'd stand out a little. Anyway, it was just one long yawn-fest … Change is definitely needed.

15 FEBRUARY 2011

Amazing news. The first opinion poll of the campaign has put Babies for Change ahead of Fianna Fáil. The full poll reads like this:

---

* Other examples of 'not the same' politicians: Joan Burton, Pol Pot, Willie O'Dea, Winston Churchill, Dick Spring, Otto von Bismarck, 'Ming' Flanagan.

FINE GAEL	40 per cent
LABOUR	31 per cent
SINN FÉIN	12 per cent
BABIES FOR CHANGE	4 per cent
FIANNA FÁIL	1 per cent
OTHERS/UNDECIDED	12 per cent

I am AWESTRUCK by this news. Lots of journalists have been ringing me up and I feel very much at the centre of today's news events. To see Babies for Change on four per cent (and, happily, not included amongst the 'Others', which is just another name for 'losers') gives me a warm, warm feeling – like an over-enthusiastic cuddle from an elderly, fat lady with large breasts. To think that a party without any real policies, without a coherent plan or strategy for the future, without any kind of infrastructure or history, without grassroots support and with no public representatives in the Dáil or on any county council in the country, is

now four times more popular than Fianna
Fáil makes me very proud indeed. I must be
doing something right!

OVERWHELMED BABY!

16 FEBRUARY 2011

Lots of articles in the paper about Babies
for Change's whopping 4 per cent show in
the opinion polls. I detect, though, most
journos feel that this is a protest vote, and
there is some surprise – or, more likely,
bewilderment – amongst them, that I am
now four times as popular as Fianna Fáil.
I admit that there *is* a 'protest vote' element
to my massive popularity, but I also think
people see in me a hope for the future; a
beacon of light in the darkness of financial
chaos. Also, I am by far the cutest candidate.

While out in the pram with Siobhan
Devlin, we bumped into George Lee having a
chat with Oscar-winning Irish actor Gabriel
Byrne in Superquinn. Both of us 'couldn't

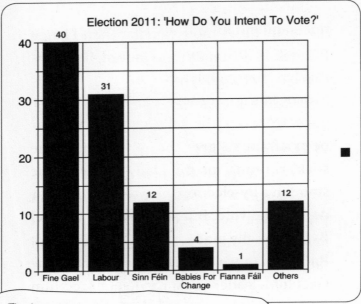

Election 2011: 'How Do You Intend To Vote?'

Party	Value
Fine Gael	40
Labour	31
Sinn Féin	12
Babies For Change	4
Fianna Fáil	1
Others	12

The first opinion poll for the 2011 general election showed Babies for Change with a healthy 3 per cent lead over Fianna Fáil. It was sometimes hard to believe we had come such a long way in such a short while.

help' overhearing their very interesting conversation. George, as everyone knows, was RTÉ's Economics Correspondent for over 50 years, before deciding to join Fine Gael. Once a member of the party, George's noble intention was to use the political process to bring about change 'from the inside'. 'The people', of course, loved the idea of this no-nonsense, 'facts and figures' guru from off the telly, who had never been afraid to give the politicians some stick, running for the Dáil – so when he stood in a by-election, he won over 100 per cent of the vote. But what he told Gabriel Byrne literally made our hair stand on end. Rather than welcoming him into the Fine Gael fold, leader Enda Kenny ignored him (although this was excusable at first, as he'd forgotten that George was now a TD, and not a troublesome journo from RTÉ). However, even when he'd remembered that George was a politician and not a reporter, Kenny would continue to give him the cold shoulder, actually hiding up a tree once at an outdoor brunch to celebrate Alan Shatter's latest successful hair-dye. 'I see you up the tree!' roared the normally mild-mannered George, but Kenny just looked the other way, and tried to cover his arse with some leaves. He was up there for several hours, apparently, staying perfectly still, as George, with typical persistence, begged him to come down and discuss a strategy to implement a series of proposed household and water charges which would not adversely affect the less well-off members of society. Eventually, the new TD was asked by security to leave.

A chilling tale.

17 FEBRUARY 2011

The problem with Siobhan Devlin isn't that she looks like Hillary Clinton, the problem is that she looks like Hillary Clinton in 1979! Bad glasses, hair too 'young' for her (occasionally in ponytails: it's 2011!), and general 'frumpy' look. I may have to have a word with her about her non-media-friendly image. If I get on the Leaders'

Debate tomorrow night on TG4 – which is still under negotiation – she's bound to be onscreen hovering around me, like the Italian lady who translates for Signor Trapattoni after the Irish football matches. If only Brand Strategy Ireland were still in operation, I could get them in to have a serious look at her.

18 FEBRUARY 2011

Watched the Leaders' Debate on Irish-language station TG4 tonight. (Like RTÉ, they didn't let me on either.) I felt my 4 per cent rating meant that I should have been there with Gilmore, Martin and Kenny. But then I consoled myself with the fact that there were probably only 6 people watching the programme. These leaders were boring enough with Pat Kenny on the *Frontline* debate, but to hear the three of them debating in Irish literally put me to sleep – for ten hours.

20 FEBRUARY 2011

Aoife Clarke is useless on the campaign walkabouts – she just sits in her pram, gurgling (admittedly with enthusiasm), with a rattle in her hand and a campaign badge stuck in her bonnet. Luckily, Siobhan Devlin has rounded up a few Babies for Change party workers to help. All between 4 and 7 years old, they are able to do non-baby stuff, such as run around very fast, hand out leaflets and climb poles to take down other parties' posters. And generally heckle politicians who aren't me.

One young boy, Charlie, had a box of crayons with him, and did some very funny drawings of me and the other candidates! I think I shall make him my official photographer. (Or rather, crayon artist.) One girl called Deirdre tripped up Ruairi Quinn from the Labour Party when we ran into him (literally) getting off the Dart at Pearse Street. Certainly, when it comes to sheer energy and youthful enthusiasm, Babies for Change is the party that delivers!

Babies for Change activist, Charlie (don't know his surname) did this funny drawing of me and Ruairi Quinn.

21 FEBRUARY 2011

Heard a very funny story while out on the 'hustings'. Apparently the People Before Profit Alliance had an initial run of 10,000 posters printed, and many of these went up on lamp posts all around Dublin, until somebody noticed that the wording on the poster read 'Profit Before People Alliance'. Surely even the most fanatical capitalist (Shane Ross!) would baulk at the idea of forming a party called the Profit Before People Alliance – especially in these days of austerity and belt-tightening?! Naturally, the printers got a stern talking-to from the uncompromising lefties, and another firm was promptly employed to produce posters with the correct wording. It's exactly the kind of funny story that would fit into a book called *Hilarious Irish Political Anecdotes*, or something like that. (Strangely, Siobhan Devlin told me quite seriously that she would consider voting for a party called the Profit Before People Alliance.* She's weird.)

---

*An early suggested slogan for my campaign from Siobhan Devlin was 'A Prophet For The People'. (A reference to me.)

22 FEBRUARY 2011

While I was canvassing outside a fruit and veg shop in Crumlin today, a man came up to me and said, 'You must be making a few quid out of all this.' I have to say, monetary gain has never been the reason I joined the world of politics. I was inspired by genuinely inspirational figures, like Nelson Mandela, Martin Luther King and Fintan O'Toole. The money which has been generated (appearance fees, donations, party membership fees, etc.) has been entrusted to Siobhan Devlin, in whom I have complete faith as my financial controller, mouthpiece, carer and confidante. I live frugally and have no interest in late nights, alcohol or serious relationships with other babies. I am totally dedicated to the cause, and, like President Barack Obama of the United States, am in politics to inspire people. (I do like the 'guilty pleasure' of a strawberry yoghurt every now and again, though. YUM!)

23 FEBRUARY 2011

More amazing news! Babies for Change
is up to 5 per cent in the polls! I seem to
have benefitted from people's sheer hatred
of Fianna Fáil, who now, unbelievably,
have dropped to minus one per cent. How
can a party actually be on MINUS ONE PER
CENT?! I'd have thought that would not be
mathematically possible, but such is the
hostility of the public to 'the soldiers of
density', that they have become the first
political party to dip below zero in terms of
public support (although, as we have seen,
as leader, Baby-Face Cowen had already
achieved this feat). I, however, am laughing
all the way to the polling station! I think
the electorate are now clearly aware that
'a spoilt vote is clearly a vote for Babies for
Change', and that a new political force has
arrived in this country.

A phrase I heard from somewhere
keeps echoing around my brain: 'RETURN

TO YOUR CONSTITUENCIES AND PREPARE FOR GOVERNMENT'. I don't actually have a constituency, but I feel that, in many ways, my dreams are coming true.

24 FEBRUARY 2011

Am continuing to get 'a good reaction on the doorsteps'. It is heartwarming to think that thousands of people all around the country are willing to spoil their vote for me. I also believe it's very important that people are *encouraged* to spoil their vote. (A TV campaign urging this course of action would be a 'breath of fresh air' among the mostly boring and redundant party political broadcasts.) It really is democracy in action. Having said that, is it fair to claim that a vote by a stupid person, too thick to be able to write a cross in a box, is a true endorsement for Babies for Change? It is a political dilemma that I find myself mulling over more and more, especially towards the end of the day. It makes me feel strangely like Winston Churchill! (Statesman-like and thoughtful.)

25 FEBRUARY 2011

Election Day! We went to spoil Siobhan Devlin's vote at a very ugly-looking national school called 'Scoil' something or other. I made QUITE an entrance in my sticker-and-bunting-festooned Battle Buggy, and it is true to say many heads were turned among the assembled media! Outside the building, there were a few Fianna Fáiler saddoes and a grim-looking Shinner straight out of central casting who, if I had asked whether a) he had a gun in his pocket or, b) was pleased to see me, would definitely have plumped for the former. There were also a few Labour-ites, still chirpy before the grim reality of coalition with Fine Gael inevitably crushes their lefty(ish) spirit. Siobhan Devlin spoilt her vote in record time, and before long we were in a local Eddie Rocket's celebrating with hamburgers (Siobhan Devlin fed me bits of bap) and ice cream.

RELAXED AND CONFIDENT BABY!

28 FEBRUARY 2011

I have not been elected to parliament. The dream – perhaps it was, after all, an impossible dream – has not come true. Disappointed, yes, but I did respectably, with an above-average number of spoilt votes counted in my constituency. Even allowing for stupid people (this is generally regarded as being between 15 and 20 per cent of the electorate), that is quite pleasing.

Suffering from understandable frustration, I employed some emergency 'therapy' to distract myself from what increasingly felt like a crushing defeat (which it wasn't). I called an extraordinary meeting of the Toy Cabinet, and, after thanking the members for their support, I had a quick reshuffle. I appointed a pack of child's playing cards (also reshuffled!) to Minister for Children and Youth Affairs, demoting Dilly to Minister for Arts, Heritage and the Gaeltacht. Showing some impressive, single-minded ruthlessness, in an initiative comparable to Hitler's infamous 'Night of the Long Knives' in 1934, I also took the hard decision to relieve Ra-Ra of her ministerial duties, and remove her from the Cabinet. We go back a long way (over a year), but there is no room for sentiment in the cut-throat world of modern politics.

My candidature was regarded in some quarters of the media as 'eccentric', but I look like the most boring Fianna Fáil 'middle-of-the-roader' compared to some of the 'Loo-Laas' who did get elected. There's one lad with a ponytail* (!) and a woman** with lively, white curly hair who dresses in

---

* Ming the Merciless, Evil Emperor of the planet Mongo, and a tireless campaigner for the legalisation of soft drugs. Presumably he'll have to give up both jobs, now that he's in the Dáil.
** Actually a man.

a flamboyant pink blouse. I'm not against democracy, but I don't think people like these should be allowed run for the Dáil.

I am rather exhausted by everything and will now attempt to have a MASSIVE sleep.

5 MARCH 2011

The last few weeks of campaigning seem to have caught up with me. I slept for four days, pausing only for eating and nappy changes. Mama says that it is time to reflect and absorb all that has happened to me, and then think of future plans. She said that William Hague of the Conservatives in England didn't become party leader until he was 16, so I have lots of time on my side.

Looking at the wider political picture, the country, rather predictably, will soon have a Fine Gael/Labour government, who will introduce fearsome austerity measures. Images flash through my mind of barefoot orphans and bedraggled adults in fingerless gloves, taking shelter from the rain in the doorways of dilapidated and crumbling tenement buildings. This is Ireland today. (And tomorrow – and possibly forever.)

DEPRESSED BABY.

About to read Vol. 1 of the McCarthy Report.

7 MARCH 2011

Siobhan Devlin is taking a well-deserved break in the Bahamas with a 'man friend'. This must be the mysterious suitor from Athlone (or surrounding area), as I recall from the time she freaked out about the lack of crèche facilities in the hotel when we were out on my book tour. Mama says that she will be gone for two weeks, so that I will be totally under the care of Mama and Dada for a change. (I hope they're up to it, and are able to get their 'arses in gear'!) I have seen so much of Siobhan Devlin that it will be strange not having her around.

8 MARCH 2011

Mama says I deserve a big present after all my hard work over the last few months. She has decided that I would like a huge teddy bear which she saw in the window of Arnotts shop. Yes, okay – what's wrong with a bit of baby-pampering? My infantile instincts are definitely to cuddle a large bear!

9 MARCH 2011

Siobhan Devlin set up a special bank account for me into which she deposited all my earnings since I became a 'marketable property'. (This is a phrase I remember her using a lot.) She promised Mama and Dada that she would give them a full breakdown of the finances once the election was over, but went off on holiday to the Bahamas without giving them the details. Mama was hoping to access some cash to buy the large teddy, but this plan has been thwarted.

12 MARCH 2011

All attempts to contact Siobhan Devlin in the Bahamas have proved fruitless.

25 MARCH 2011

Siobhan Devlin is on the run!! Mama and Dada finally found out what hotel in the Bahamas she was staying in, but apparently she checked out three days ago and didn't leave a forwarding address. Mama, in something of a panic, suggested to Dada that maybe Interpol could be called in to investigate.

26 MARCH 2011

There are more disturbing and sensational developments every day. Siobhan Devlin took ALL the money out of 'our' bank account before she left for the Bahamas. A sum of €20,000 has been mentioned. Lordy! Dada was enraged, saying, 'I told you to watch your back with Siobhan Devlin!' Aha, WATCH your back …

30 MARCH 2011

What has Siobhan Devlin done with all the cash? Mama remarked that 20,000 smackers would certainly be enough to transform her from a Hillary Clinton 1979-era frump merchant into a pleasing older-woman Meryl Streep-type. It would also be handy for Siobhan Devlin to have a completely new look, if she wants to stay one step ahead of Interpol. (Since nobody can find any actual photographs of Siobhan Devlin, Interpol have used a picture of Hillary Clinton circa 1979 on their 'Wanted' poster.) Who would have imagined that my humble childminder would end up living the life of a notorious on-the-run international criminal, like Carlos the Jackal? My theory is that she genuinely doesn't care about her looks, and is at this very moment swanning around the Caribbean hot-spots with her Athlone lover-man, sipping margaritas and dipping into the warm waters. Who knows?! She seems to have disappeared off the face of the earth.

9 FEBRUARY 2012

I am 2 years old today. A lot has changed since my last diary entry in March of last year. I have grown up a little (literally).

WANTED

DEAD OR ALIVE

*No photo of suspect available. 'Lookalike' used for identification purposes.

SIOBHAN DEVLIN

Please contact INTERPOL today

Interpol's surprisingly 'Wild West'-themed Wanted poster for my 'on-the-run' nanny and sometime child whisperer, Siobhan Devlin.

Maybe I look at things differently. Perhaps my youthful indignation and energy has dimmed somewhat. I am less of a 'firebrand'. Didn't somebody once say, 'Isn't it funny how you get more right-wing when you get older'?* I wouldn't say I am 'more right-wing', but I am less inclined to join street protests and attempt to occupy government buildings with a bunch of tent-dwelling, anti-globalisation hippies (possibly smelly too).

Of course, I am still desperately unhappy at the dreadful state of the country, but maybe, like so much of the population, a degree of apathy has set in for me now. One feels a certain despair that Ireland will, well, always be Ireland and there is NOTHING that one can do about it. There is a phrase that my father likes to use, which has a definite ring of truth to it: 'We're permanently f***ed.' Despite his gruff exterior, he is a wise man in many ways.

* I did, on page 75.

My career in politics leading up to the election last year exhausted me more than I realised at the time. After the Siobhan Devlin debacle, Mama felt it was time for me to be a 'proper' baby once more, and return to life within the bosom of the family. It was nice to just do the simple things again: gurgle, dribble, toddle about and bump into things. For perhaps the first time in my life, I began to enjoy myself. All activists must take a break at some stage from the stresses of political life. Shane Ross goes bungee jumping; David McWilliams reads tarot cards; Matt Cooper regularly climbs Mount Everest; and Fintan has his gardening column in *The Irish Times*.

I still write my blog, but these days it tends to be more about programmes I enjoy on television, such as the adventures of Iggle Piggle and Upsy Daisy in *In the Night Garden*, and *Peppa Pig* and *Mrs Brown's Boys*. Maybe some time in the future I will return to the hurly-burly of politics, but for the moment I am just enjoying the everyday experience of being extremely young.

In late October last year, Interpol finally caught up with Siobhan Devlin. She was living in a crack house in Amsterdam where she had been working as a prostitute. She had gone through the €20,000 in record time, and had spent a substantial whack of it on a wedding to her Athlone boyfriend in Las Vegas, where they were married by an Elvis lookalike. Now divorced, she is currently in custody in the Dutch capital, awaiting extradition. In context, €20,000 is a mere trifle compared to the millions owed by the bankers, so I have a certain amount of sympathy for Siobhan Devlin. After all, she was just doing something which is absolutely instinctive in the average Irish person – ripping somebody else off. (It is worth noting that my new childminder is Norwegian.)

* * *

About a week ago, myself and Mama and Dada were out walking in Dublin city centre. We were about to cross the road, when an old tramp approached us – suddenly arriving, it seemed to me, from out of nowhere. His grey hair was matted, and he wore a long, dirty beige coat, tied at the waist with a length of twine. He was unshaven, and his breath smelled of beer. He thrust his hand out in front of Dada. I noticed it was shaking, and the nails were unusually long. Black, ugly dirt was firmly lodged in the places where nail met fingertip. In a plaintive, yet strong Dublin accent, he beseeched us, 'Could you give me a bit of a dig-out?'

Dada obviously felt sorry for the sad old wretch, so he searched around in his pocket and extracted a €2 coin. He handed it to the poor fellow, who, in a half-cackle, half-wheeze, mumbled something inaudible, before stumbling across the road, narrowly missing being hit by a No. 16 bus. Dada and Mama looked at him go. The encounter had obviously stirred something deep inside of them.

But there was more to it than that. Mama and Dada seemed to be familiar with the old tramp. But how could my parents have come across somebody like that in the course of their respectable, comfortable middle-class lives? It didn't make sense. Yet Mama began to smile slowly. Her recognition of the old tramp had fully sunk in. 'Do you know who that was?' she said to me. I certainly didn't recognise the unfortunate creature, and I was plainly staggered that he would be an acquaintance of our family. Mama patted me on the head, slowly, and bent down to whisper in my ear. 'That, my child, was Bertie Ahern.'

10 FEBRUARY 2012

It actually wasn't Bertie Ahern. It was just someone who looked a bit like him. Still, it's a good metaphor for the country.

ACKNOWLEDGEMENTS

Katie would like to thank Faith O'Grady, who became her new agent/minder after her previous agent/minder went on the run. More thanks to Ciara Considine for suggesting she write a book after spotting her wearing a 'Bertie Ahern Ruined My Country' T-shirt. Also, thank you to the baby carers at Hachette Books Ireland.